18 Months in the Spanking Scene

Anna J Skye

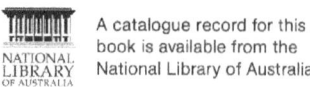 A catalogue record for this book is available from the National Library of Australia

Copyright © 2021 Anna J Skye
All rights reserved.
ISBN-13: 978-1-922727-06-0

Linellen Press
265 Boomerang Road
Oldbury, Western Australia
www.linellenpress.com.au

Dedication

Dedicated to all the brave spankers and spankees out there who have dared to follow their fetish dreams.
Have fun.

Acknowledgements

I am very grateful to Robin, Blue, Jeremy, Mr Spanker-at-Heathrow, Nick Turner, Matt James and numerous other spankers for allowing their spanking stories to come to print, and for easing me gently (and sometimes not so gently) into the spanking scene during my debut year and a half as a spankee.

I'm especially grateful to Russell de Mille, for taking a good deal of time to impart so much knowledge about spanking parties. His corrections and suggestions to my original description of spanking parties have correctly emphasised how much fun they can be.

I really appreciate the help and patience shown to me by my publisher Helen Iles from Linellen Press in Australia. Her friendly professionalism, experienced knowledge of publishing and sense of humour has definitely made the process of writing and publishing this book more enjoyable.

I shall always be deeply grateful to my parents for giving me such a privileged start in life, and for being there for me, no matter what. They are blissfully unaware of many events in my life that either befell me or that I undertook voluntarily. I have never found the courage to tell them about many of these events, some of which are described in this book. My parents have their values, and I respect them enough to leave them in peace and not try to justify what would have been to them disappointing and outrageous activities.

*****

Most names and locations referred to have been changed to protect the identity of individuals.

Contents

Dedication iii

Acknowledgements v

Contents vii

Foreword 3

Prologue 5

Chapter 1 - Secure Beginnings 8

Chapter 2 - Into the Red 10

Chapter 3 - Preparing to be Spanked 16

Chapter 4 - My First Spanker 24

Chapter 5 - My Youngest Spanker 37

Chapter 6 - Why Spanking? 41

Chapter 7 - Party-Lover Jeremy 50

Chapter 8 - My First Caning 58

Chapter 9 - Out of the Blue 64

Chapter 10 - Boyfriends and Babies 95

Chapter 11 - Spanking Parties 99

Chapter 12 - The Problem with Novices 111

Chapter 13 - Fetishes 116

Chapter 14 - Canes, Crops, Slippers and Hairbrushes 125

Chapter 15 - Taking Stock 132

Chapter 16 - The Studio 135

Chapter 17 - Dating and Spanking 138

Chapter 18 - Office Work 152

Chapter 19 - A Step Too Far 159

Chapter 20 - Welsh Rarebit 168

Chapter 21 - Love and Spanking 179

Chapter 22 - Promoting the Book with my New Assistant Dom 199

Chapter 23 - What Now? 217

References 219

*'There is no greater agony
than bearing an untold story inside you.'*

Maya Angelou
I Know Why the Caged Bird Sings.

Foreword

My life has not been what I thought it would be. Experiencing an extremely happy and easy childhood, I assumed I would achieve everything I wanted in life, which was simply to have a loving marriage and two children. I've achieved neither, but along the way have had a few adventures as well as disasters. At the age of 59, I found I was sometimes itching to tell people about them, but feared a reaction of shock and/or disappointment, so I began writing my first autobiography, *Out of the Red*, to 'get it out there'.

Halfway through writing the first autobiography, I started a new career as a spankee to pay off some debts. I mentioned this new activity to the publishers, who jumped at the idea, declaring that it would probably help sell the book. The result was that the book rather changed tack halfway through, and the second half was dominated by my spanking exploits. The publishers added the sub-title '*Spanked for Profit and Pleasure*', and by clever marketing the book made the 'bestsellers' list on *Amazon*. But, of course, most people bought it for the spanking stories and were disappointed when they first had to wade through pages of personal history, which was only interesting to me and a few loyal friends. What's more, I left out many spanking stories in the first book for fear of overloading the reader with the same subject.

So I decided to write a second book purely about my eighteen months as a spankee, and this time every salacious detail fills the pages. I make no apology that some of the spanking stories were also told in the first book, but most were not told in such detail.

The first book was written six years ago, so hopefully readers of this second book might either not have read the first book at all, or might have forgotten those stories.

Prologue

Room 132, he had said. Go past reception and turn right down the corridor. I arrived at the door and took a few seconds to compose myself before knocking.

The door opened and a very tall, well-dressed man in his early sixties stood holding the door open for me, smiling.

'I'm hoping it's you,' he said.

'And I'm hoping it's you,' I said, smiling back.

He had answered my spankee advertisement and, during the initial phone conversation, we had quickly determined that we were both 'safe', and suitable for a session. We had had one previous session, which had gone well, so we were both keen to have a second session. This time it had to be held in a hotel near Heathrow, a two-hour drive for both of us, and midway between our homes.

I walked into the room with a growing sense of excitement. How hard would the spanking be this time? When would we start? How naked would I be? What position would he place me in? What implements, if any, would he use?

I sat on the bed, he on the chair opposite me. After some small chit-chat, he suddenly said, 'I'm going to spank you now – come here,' and he beckoned to me. 'You were 45 minutes late last time and I never punished you for it. Stand there.' He pointed to the floor just by his left leg.

I walked over to him, and before I could take up the allotted position by his leg he pulled me over his knee and started caressing my bottom over my yellow dress. He gave me a few initial light slaps to warm up my bottom. I was to learn that this is customary practice in spanking circles. It mitigates the sting from the firmer slaps that nearly always follow. Then he pulled up my dress, then my petticoat, and started feeling my buttocks over my yellow knickers. He pulled down my knickers to my knees as I lay over his lap, paused a moment to look at my reddening bottom, as if surveying his handiwork, and started spanking me again, harder this time.

It was an engineered excuse to discipline me, of course. In most social circles, an apology would have been accepted. When you're a spankee, the rules are somewhat different.

After about five minutes of continuous spanking with a fairly firm hand, he suddenly stopped. 'Right,' he said. 'Shall we go and have a drink, or would you like something to eat?'

I found this sort of interaction rather strange in my first few weeks as a spankee. Some of the spankers would even ask me mid-spanking, 'How are you, by the way? Is it not too hard for you?' They would come out of spanker-spankee mode for a few minutes, reverting to the charming character that greeted me at the beginning of the session, and then just as suddenly tell me, 'You're a naughty girl, and you deserve a good thrashing.' Then their 'normal' personality would be gone, replaced by the not-so-nice, dominant spanker personality.

I hadn't expected guys to be nice to me. I had assumed that they would treat me like a prostitute and look down on me, bully me or patronise me. It had been a leap of faith, and I was constantly surprised. In fact, apart from one man, the first as it happens (although I think that had much to do with my inexperienced behaviour), all thirty or so spankers I met were friendly, polite and gentlemanly. Quite a few wanted to date me. I was totally naked with some, bent over chairs and beds, red bottom raised, my lips on display, but I had nothing but humour, respect, friendship and, above all, gratitude for having such a spankable bottom, and for sharing it with the spanking fraternity.

Some admired me for daring to enter the world of spanking at such a late age; I was 57. But I did have an exceptionally young body, partly due to family genes, but also due to having taken part in sports from a very young age, and keeping slim. Some of the spankers said it was the best bottom they'd ever spanked.

The other factor in my favour was that most of the spankers were in their late 50s and early 60s, so didn't view me as old, but simply one of them.

Mr Spanker-at-Heathrow and I went down into the lounge of the hotel. As I sat down, I could feel my bottom smarting, with a degree of satisfaction.

We chatted like old friends about our families, work and our previous spanking experiences. I looked around the lounge at other customers, wondering if they could tell that I was a spankee with my client. I was wearing a knee-length yellow summer dress, under a coat; not a bra and thong with a label saying 'Spank Me,' but I still felt the thrill of deception.

After one gin and tonic for me and a half of lager for him, which I paid for to his great surprise (he told me most spankees expect their spankers to pay for all expenses), he suggested continuing the session.

As soon as we were back in the room, the friendly, chatty individual all but vanished. He pushed me over the bed, raised my dress, pulled my knickers down again, and, standing beside the bed, spanked me hard with his hand for about five minutes, spanking one buttock about three times, and then the other, and then returning to the first buttock again. He never spanked across both buttocks at the same time, as this can hurt the vagina.

Then he sat down on the chair and ordered me to change into my short silk nightie, with no underwear, and place myself on all fours on the bed. He watched me as I got undressed. When I had taken up my position on the bed, he got up and came round the bed and stood beside me. He caressed me between my legs for a few minutes under the nightie. Then he pulled the nightie up to expose my bottom and asked me if I was OK.

'Sure,' I answered, waiting expectantly for the oncoming punishment. With that, he took off his belt and proceeded to thrash me about twenty times across my bare buttocks.

Chapter 1

Secure Beginnings

I was brought up by well-off, white British upper-middle-class parents to be a nice young lady who knew how to behave at cocktail parties and dinner parties. For the first eighteen years of my life, I lived with my parents and two sisters in a fairly large four-bedroomed detached house with a big, sloping garden, surrounded by other large houses with even bigger gardens, at the top of a quiet hill on the edge of a quiet country town in the West Country.

I was educated from the age of seven to eighteen in a 'High School for Girls' grammar school. I was obedient and fairly repressed and, above all, wanted to be accepted by friends and to do well in school and sports. This I largely achieved. I don't remember ever feeling worried that I wouldn't make the grade in school, either on a popularity front or academic level.

Three girls in my class were subtly vying to be my 'best friend' and, although I favoured one of them, and had the lack of grace to tell my current best friend that I wanted the other girl to take her place (I shudder to think of such unkindness today), I subsequently tried not to overtly choose between them or offend them, as I rather liked the attention. We were part of a group of six girls who spent time together in and out of school. I also spent time with two girls in my neighbourhood until they were whisked away to boarding school, much to my indignation.

I thought this was a normal life. I made friends easily. I was pretty, blonde, good at sports and had a handsome boyfriend from the age of fifteen to eighteen. I didn't realise just what a pampered existence it all was, which is probably a good definition of security – never having to think about your life, or whether it's on the right course, or whether you're accepted in your chosen circles, let alone where the next meal is coming from, or whether you will have a roof over your head that night, like millions of children nowadays throughout the world.

Little did I know that friends can sometimes be hard to find, and loneliness can envelop you to the point where you even begin to envy two people walking down the street together.

Back then family life was all my parents wanted. Mum stayed at home and looked after the needs of three growing girls while Dad went to the office a mile away. On Saturday afternoons he played tennis and we girls went riding. On Sunday mornings, we were made to go to church (which I hated) and on Sunday afternoons, we were made to go for a walk (which I also hated).

My parents never made any reference to what they hoped would be our futures, apart from my mother sometimes saying she hoped she would have many grandchildren. I took it for granted that I would provide her with some of those grandchildren. I grew up with the same simple ambition – to get married and be a stay-at-home mum of two children. I never wanted to go out to work or have a career. Not for a single day.

I'm pretty sure my parents would not have chosen 'spankee' as a career for me.

Chapter 2

Into the Red

It was a summer morning in 2011 and my husband of fourteen years, Pen, had asked me to ring his office and tell them he felt ill, so that he could go and race in his Formula Ford car at the nearby race track. He rushed around the house, packing items in a large day bag. I wondered what film we were going to watch that evening on his return, and called down from the upstairs landing to ask if he had any preferences. Despite being very late, and panicking that he wouldn't have packed all the right gear, he took time to dash up the stairs and say, 'I don't mind. You choose.' Then he raced downstairs, picked up his bag and was gone. No time for the usual goodbye kiss.

That was the last time I saw him alive.

Pen had been having chest pains the week before. His blood pressure had shot up to 180, and he had been put on statins. He should also have been told not to exert himself too much until his blood pressure had dropped to normal levels. Knowing his love for motor racing, he probably would have ignored such advice anyway.

He was driving his racing car round a bend in the race track that day, heart pounding, adrenaline coursing through his veins, when one of his arteries, furred by years of smoking and pizzas, ruptured. He died instantly. A race steward saw Pen's head go backwards, as his car trundled off the track and came to rest in a nearby field. Luckily no other driver was hurt. An air ambulance was called but was soon sent away as he was pronounced dead at the scene. It was 11.03 am.

I was told the news by the police at around 11.30 that morning, when they came round to the house and I heard the proverbial knock on the door. I had been talking to Pen three hours earlier. In a split second, my partner of nineteen years had been taken from me. We had had no children since I had had the menopause at thirty-seven, the same year I met him. We had had eight unsuccessful IVF cycles, which had been expensive and devastatingly disappointing.

So on that day in August, when I was told of his death, I had never felt so utterly alone. As the police officer in my sitting room was telling me what he knew of the events, and with my mind in deep shock and turmoil, I found myself wondering bizarrely whom I would watch the film with that evening.

I didn't go into work for six weeks, but having a void to fill I did keep working remotely from home as a software developer, my job of twenty-five years at that point. The hardest part was having no one to chat to at the end of the day about the little everyday things that had happened during the day. There was no one to do nothing with, as they say. Strangely, I didn't sink into depression. But my marriage had had many problems, and although I still loved him, I had also started to resent his frequent lies and the fact that I had had to pay nearly all the bills since our marriage began, as he never seemed to have any money.

He'd had several jobs during the marriage but none of them seemed to bring in enough money to allow him to help pay for the bills, although he did often pay for the shopping. This consisted mostly of pizzas and ready-made meals since neither of us was any good at, or had any interest in, cooking.

He hated the fact that I had a better-paid, grander-sounding job than him. I had been a software developer for six years when I met him. He had just finished his law degree as a mature student and hoped to become a solicitor. But he only obtained a 2:2 and was rejected before even reaching the interview stage by all firms to which he applied. After a few weeks, he gave up applying. If neighbours asked him about his job, he fed them a very convincing line about a home-run property company.

I played tennis, badminton and volleyball regularly, partly to keep fit, but also because I loved all three sports. I was quite good at all three, and it was my main source of social life. Pen did no exercise. He also smoked. He did try to give up twice, and I believed that he had succeeded the last time, but after he died, I found packets of cigarettes, one already opened, in his car. In the glove compartment were mints, which he must have used to disguise his smoky breath from me. Unbeknown to both of us, his arteries were furring up and his blood pressure was becoming dangerously high.

Even though he didn't earn much at the car sales job he eventually landed, he strangely seemed to have enough money to pursue his favourite pastime – motor racing. To justify this to me, he always insisted his motor racing didn't cost any more than the petrol down to the race track, and that anyway he was trying to sell his racing car. I found out after he died that he had taken no steps to sell the car, and was purely keeping me from asking too many nagging questions.

He had also stayed in Premier Inns overnight when he raced, whereas he told me he slept in a friend's lorry at no charge at the site. He had claimed he had been given the car as a gift from a rich friend who wanted to try motor racing as a hobby himself and needed Pen to accompany him in another car to show him the ropes. Looking back now, I wonder if that was another lie. Perhaps he just borrowed the money to buy a car for himself.

However much I resented his inability to pay for household bills, I was glad for his sake that he had a hobby. He was good at it, and I know it made him feel successful at something. He did sometimes admit that it wasn't right that I should pay for everything, and I know he felt guilty for not contributing. I wanted so badly to believe that his chosen sport didn't cost very much.

After his death, I started trawling through his papers. I found many photos of women wearing titillating underwear in spankable poses. There were lists of women's names, with their phone numbers, and scribbled notes to them describing what spanking positions he and a mate of his wanted to try out. Quite ironic, given my later activity. How could he have afforded this when there was the electricity bill to pay? Pen and I had, in fact, experimented with spanking, but tired of it quickly as we were unfamiliar with the myriad of spanking implements available and the use of punishment scenarios, which I was so often to encounter within the spanking community.

I found that he had run up huge debts on five or six credit cards without my knowledge, to the tune of about £20,000. He had frequently gone for a drink with his best mate. Now I saw that he had bought drinks with a credit card, refusing to admit to his friend that he didn't even have enough money for a round of drinks. Luckily these debts would die with him, as they were in his name, but he had been obviously battling to meet the monthly payments, which had prevented him from helping me with the bills. It's doubtful he would have helped me anyway, even if he had had the funds.

About six weeks before his death, he had come to me and asked me to help him consolidate his debts, without telling me the final figure. He said he wasn't able to take out a loan as his credit rating was so poor. He said he would make monthly payments to me to cover my payments for the loan.

So I took out a Tesco loan for £20,000 and handed him a cheque. I was so pleased that he seemed to be genuinely making an effort to get rid of all his debts that I never checked what he did with this money, or whether he was making payments to cover my payments. And to this day, there has never been a trace of it in his bank account, and he never set up any payments to cover my monthly payments.

After his death, I was saddled with this £20,000 loan, which was still in my name. As I sat there, finding more evidence of his deception and lies, I started to realise that I'd had a lucky escape. I reckoned he would probably have made us lose the house. I started to resent him still further for putting me in this situation while still loving him and missing him deeply.

Over the previous few years, I'd had to fork out about £18,000 for fertility treatment, due to early menopause, which had made quite a dent in my coffers and was still having a knock-on effect, making it impossible to pay anything but the minimum payment towards the £20,000 figure. I also had a £160,000 mortgage in my name. It had started at £100,000 when we bought the house, but Pen had re-mortgaged twice to help his finances. I had supported the re-mortgaging as each time I had been convinced by his remonstrations that he would never be in debt again.

I also found out to my horror that he had cancelled his life insurance policy about six months before he died. I was paying all the bills but had left him to pay his own life insurance of £20 a month. With hindsight, that was the only bill I should have paid, in that I was going to be the sole beneficiary. If he had kept it going until he died, I would have received £54,000. I had coincidentally asked him a short time before his death whether he was still paying the premiums, and he had answered with feigned indignation, 'oh yes!'

A friend of mine was also married to a liar. After they split up, she realised just how much lying had become a way of life for him. The more he lied, the more he had to lie, to the point where he almost believed the lies himself. As I listened to her, I recognised so much of her husband's behaviour in Pen.

Pen had a willing accomplice for his lies – me. I was desperate to prove to myself that I had chosen a good husband, that eventually he wouldn't have to lie, and that we would form a strong bond based on respect and honesty. So I didn't always pull him up on inconsistencies in his stories, turning a blind eye to fibs that I tried to justify to myself weren't worth arguing about.

I also still loved him and kept telling myself that once he had a good job, and once I'd had the longed-for child, he would stop having to lie, and we would be fine.

But during the dark days immediately after his death, through tears of deep resentment, anger and sadness, I decided that he didn't deserve any more of my time. I wasn't going to waste my life mourning him to the point of putting my life on hold for a day longer. Two weeks after he died, I signed up for an online dating site.

Chapter 3

Preparing to be Spanked

Fifteen months and twenty-two men later, I was no nearer finding a partner. I was also not making much headway into paying off the £20,000 debt he had unwittingly landed on my shoulders.

I couldn't face the idea of having an evening job on top of my day job as a software developer. I also wouldn't contemplate going cap in hand to my parents. They had given me such a good start in life – a loving home, secure surroundings, a good education, not to mention a sizeable lump sum towards my first home about twenty years previously. How could I then turn round and say I was in debt and could they bail me out?

*****

One evening I noticed my bottom in the bathroom mirror. It was a pretty good size and shape. I fetched a slipper from the bedroom and gave myself a few whacks with it. Pah – that was nothing. I could take a good spanking, I reckoned. I wondered if I could find a way of being spanked for money. I imagined that men might put me over their knee fully clothed, give me about ten playful slaps and then I would be on my merry way home. Very occasionally, some of the more daring ones might raise my skirt and slap me over my knickers.

I smile now at my childlike naivety.

I googled 'spanking', and among the results was a site advertising for girls to be spanked. I entered the site and felt my heart rate increase. This, to me, felt like a dark world, veering on prostitution. It was probably dangerous and sordid, and I didn't know if I was brave enough.

I found the home page and saw a note on it that said a website could be created free of charge for would-be spankees. I noticed with relief that spankees, as opposed to escorts on the same site, were offering 'fun spanking games with no sex or sexual contact.' It went on to say that to make any sexual move against the spankee without their consent could be construed as indecent assault in the eyes of the law and perpetrators could be prosecuted. It emphasised that spankees did feel pain, so the limits they set on how hard and with what implement they could be spanked had to be respected. It also said that some spankees also offered sexual services and some escorts could take a firm spanking, but this should never be assumed.

I wondered what the catch was, and whether the web developer demanded sex in exchange for the website. There was a contact email. I thought it could do no harm to ask, so I wrote there and then, before I could change my mind. I sent off the email – and my heart rate rose even further. I asked about rates, what spankers expect, and how dangerous it was for girls, while not believing that I could actually be doing this.

Within a day or so, I received a friendly reply from a man called Duncan. The spelling and grammar were immaculate, which surprised me. I thought I might hear from some backstreet pimp with no education. He confirmed that he could produce a web page for free if I gave him some text and some photos of myself in whatever pose I wanted. He said he could put me in touch with an existing, experienced spankee, who could tell me the advantages and pitfalls. I asked if I could charge for being spanked, and he said he thought it was about £100 an hour. For doing something I quite liked anyway? My interest was piqued. He gave me the email of a girl called Emeralda, which I took to be her spankee name.

I was encouraged by Duncan's friendly helpfulness and the

seeming accessibility of the spanking world, so I decided to venture further and email my fellow spankee. She was also friendly and replied within a day. She said that clients were mostly married men in their 50s and above, who just wanted a 'bottom to spank'. They were normally not interested in a relationship. She charged £100 an hour.

'*Do they spank hard?*' I asked, '*and do they take your knickers down? Do they ever follow you home, or demand sex, or become violent?*'

'*No, they don't spank hard,*' she replied. '*Yes, they nearly always take your knickers down. They've never followed me home. Some of them do ask if they can have sex, or they might ask for sexual favours, but they don't pursue it when I refuse.*'

'*Where do you do it?*'

'*Mostly their homes, or my home. I met my first client at a pub and then followed him to his house. I was absolutely terrified. But it was fine and now he's a regular.*'

'*Do they stop when you say stop?*'

'*Yes, although I've heard that just occasionally spankers don't stop when spankees ask them to stop.*'

This last answer worried me somewhat. I found out a few months after this that Emeralda had been in a hotel room with a spanker, who had started to cane her with her permission. After her normal quota of strokes, she had asked him to stop, but he decided he hadn't had his money's worth, and continued to thrash her as she writhed on the floor, trying to escape him. Somehow she managed to get hold of her mobile and rang a male friend in the spanking scene, who spoke to the guy and managed to calm him down. She hadn't mentioned this to me during our initial email conversation. Presumably, she didn't want to put me off.

'*Do you get any cranks?*'

'*No, I haven't so far. Some will email you and after a while it's obvious they are not interested or brave enough to meet you. So I just say to them, "If you'd like to arrange a session, just email me again."*'

Before I could stop myself, I remarked to her, '*Gosh. You sound so* normal.'

I realised afterwards with regret that that sounded patronising. 'Normal' to whom? I had meant normal by my own standards. Who gave me the right to pre-judge people when I knew nothing about them or this spanking world? Probably along with the rest of the world, I had a lot to learn.

'*Lol. Of course I'm normal!*' she answered generously, without any hint of offence taken.

I went back to Duncan and said I would like him to go ahead and create me a web page. I would send him some photos. One thing bothered me.

'*I'm 57. Are clients going to want to spank me when there must be so many other younger spankees available?*'

'Oh, don't you worry,' he replied kindly, '*Many spankers are in their sixties. They quite like older spankees since they can relate to them more easily. I'm nearly 70, so you are all young to me! One thing I would recommend is to put a sort of disclaimer on the bottom of your web page, saying that you will not perform sexual favours.*'

I couldn't wait to start taking photos of myself in various rude poses. I looked at some of the other girls' photos on their websites. They were all quite different from each other, with all shapes and sizes of bottoms being displayed. Some pages showed faceless men's hands about to slap bare bottoms. Some spankees were alone and completely naked, bent over a chair or table. Some were standing but bent over themselves at the waist, almost fully dressed, with their skirt raised, knickers round their knees while an anonymous male hand could be seen holding a strap and about to strike an already reddened bottom facing the camera. Some showed their faces, and I envied them their candour and openness. There was no way I was showing my face, in case I was recognised. Although no doubt if anyone had recognised me, they may not have wanted to admit they were dipping into spanking sites.

I put my Instamatic on ten seconds delay, took down my jeans to below my knees, pulled my lacy knickers half way down my buttocks to what I decided was a very tempting position, and bent over the armchair in my sitting room. The first twenty photos or so were awful. I was off-centre or my thighs or bottom looked too fat due to being too near the camera, or one buttock was missing from the photo. So I dimmed the lights, took up position again and this time produced sexier photos. I pulled my knickers all the way down to my knees and took a few more. Then I took my knickers off, put on a white, lacy, summer dress, pulled it up to reveal half a bare bottom and took the final photos. These photos were sexy. In the half-light, I looked rather innocent in white lace but naughty enough to be spanked. I was ready for my life as a rookie spankee.

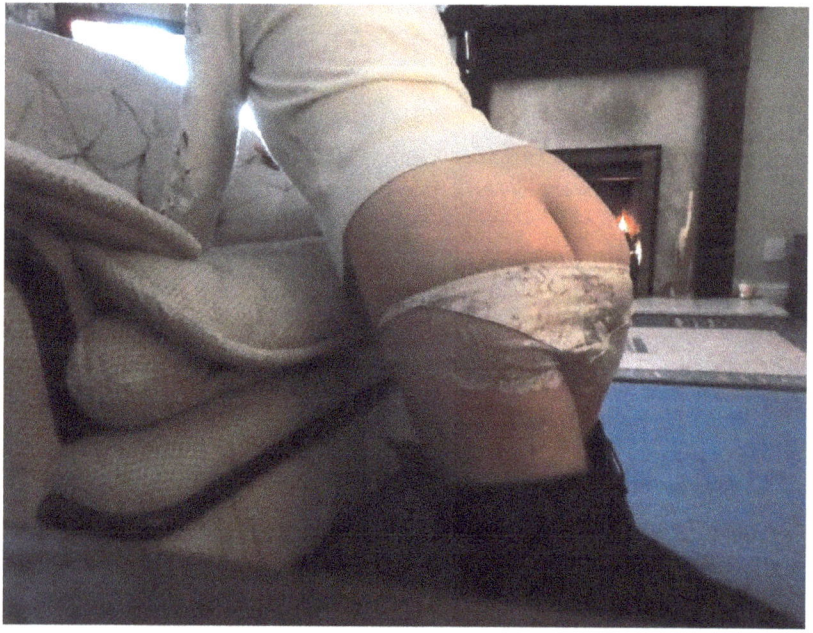

First photo sent to Duncan for my spankee web page

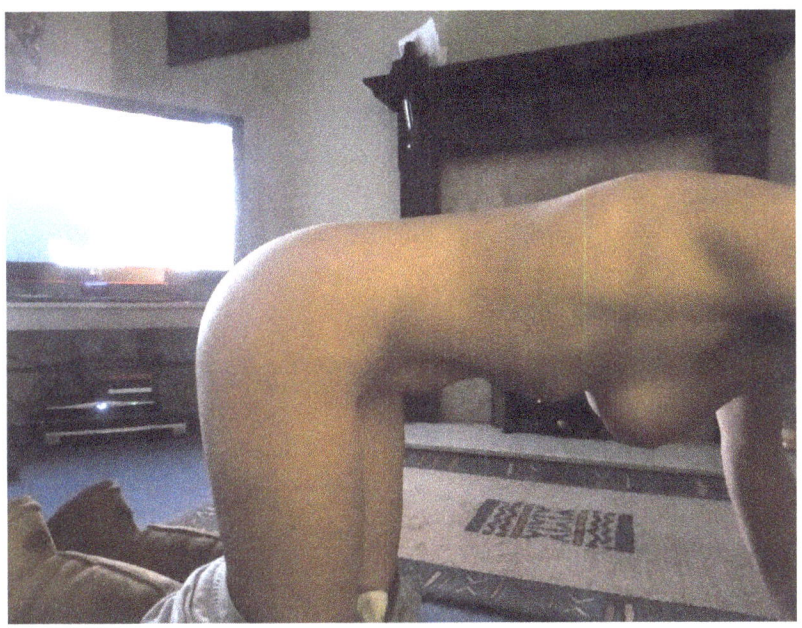

Second photo I took for Duncan but never sent as I decided it was too revealing. Had I known at this stage that I would later quite happily go naked for clients, I probably would have included it.

The web page was ready within a few days. The photo chosen by the web developer was the one in the white dress. This photo has unfortunately since been lost. It showed the spankee name I had chosen (Lily-Rose) and an email address, specially created for spanking activities, at the bottom. I noticed that my name was tagged as a new entry in the list of spankees, as many spankers like 'virgin' spankees. There was also a full-length feature page, where they chose certain spankees one by one to give them a boost in clients. There I was, in all my glory. Knickerless, in a sweet, white, lace dress. My accompanying text included that I had a university degree, kept my body fit and slim by playing badminton and tennis for much of my life, and stated that I did not take drugs and would not perform sexual favours.

So this was it. I was about to display my bottom to the world.

*****

My main web page has since been taken down by my request, but a friend in the spanking scene told me recently that, unbeknown to me, a sister webpage was set up for me at the same time as the main one, written in much more flowery, titillating language, using two of my other photos. He kindly sent me a copy of the page, even though it's no longer viewable online. My spankee name mentioned in the text had been made into a web link, where brazen girls were proudly and boldly parading their astoundingly sexy bottoms, naked bodies and faces for all to see in photos and videos. My two little faceless photos looked very demure beside them:

*****

> *The second spankee to be found in the Midlands area is Lily-Rose who is a mature lady who enjoys being spanked. Many spankees leave the scene, while still in their twenties and thirties. On this site, we are often asked by gentlemen if there are any spankees who are a bit older.*

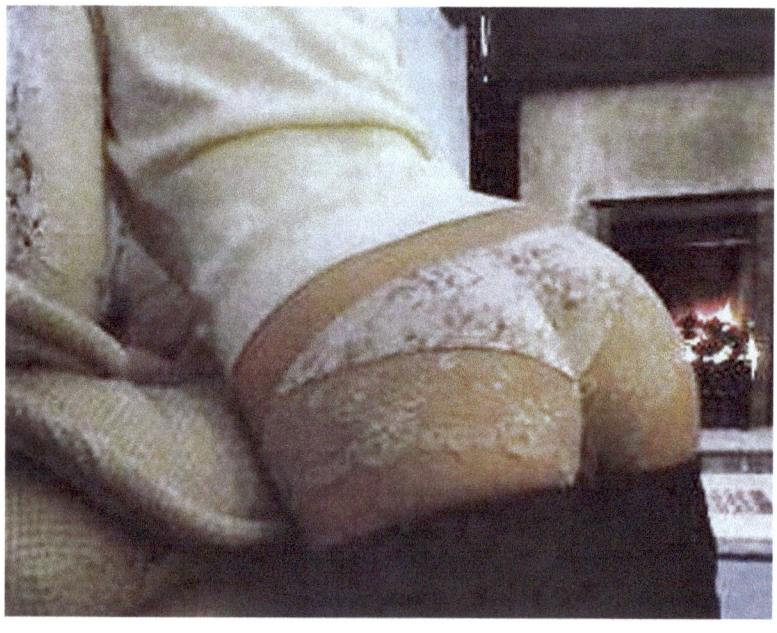

Well, Lily-Rose is a rather special mature lady. Several times a week, she can be found dancing, or playing tennis or badminton, so has a slim and toned body. As the picture shows, she has a shapely waist and a delightfully rounded bottom.

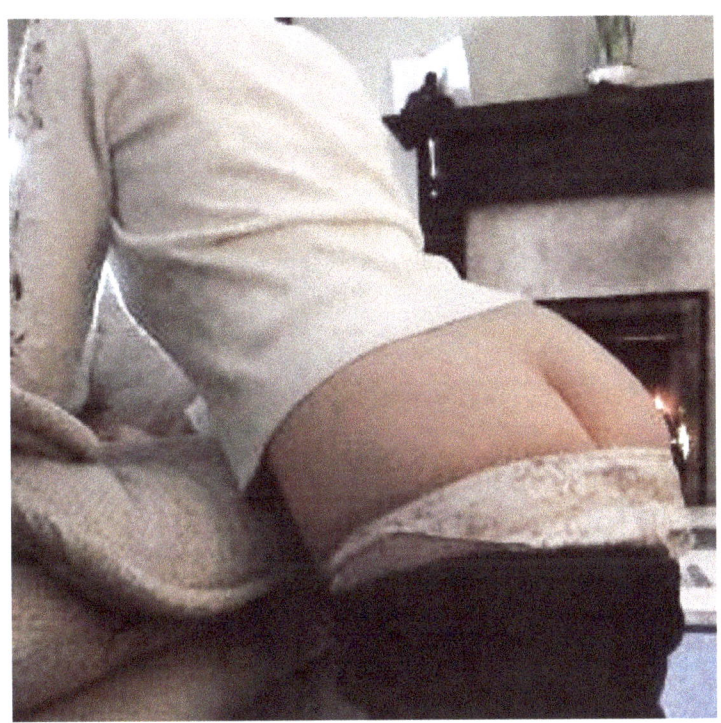

Lily-Rose says that for a first encounter, a gentleman can spank her, as well as give her the slipper, which she thoughtfully provides. Now the slipper is an implement as old as spanking itself and is much favoured by many gentlemen. They can now pull down Lily-Rose's lace-trimmed panties, and in the traditional manner, vigorously apply the slipper to Lily-Rose's bare bottom.

*****

Chapter 4

My First Spanker

I waited two days – nothing. On the third day, I received about three or four replies. Polite, well-written emails from men mostly in their fifties and sixties, just like Duncan had predicted. But I was surprised to see that one man was forty and another was in his twenties, yet they still wanted to spank a much older woman when there must have been many spankees nearer their own age available.

The general format seemed to be to introduce themselves, give a quick synopsis of their spanking experience and preferences, and then state what sort of session they would like with me.

The following three emails have been taken verbatim from these initial requests, including spelling and grammar mistakes. All names have been changed to protect identities. I found out later that the term 'the scene' means the general spanking community and their activities, the acronym 'CP' means 'corporal punishment', and is fairly synonymous with 'the scene'; 'player' means someone who takes part in CP; OTK means 'over the knee', which normally means a hand-spanking, and 'vanilla' is the word given to someone not in the CP world.

---oOo---

'Hello Lily-Rose,

I've seen your ad on spankee ******.

My name is Z, I'm a 50yr old male and live on the Stsaffs/Derbys border in the Midlands.

I am totally genuine and would be keen to hear from you with a view to a session together. I've been an occassional player in CP for a few years but struggle to find the time, like role-play, secretary or school scenarios. I enjoy putting a naughty lady over my kneee and giving her the spanking she deserves. I am much into the fun and mutual pleasure of it all rather than pain.

So come on let me ut some colour into your cheeks!

Z'

---oOo---

'Hi Lily-Rose:

My name is F. I am a 40 years old, well educated, clean, well built, good sense of humour and very respectful.

I have seen your ad on Spankee ******* and am very interested in meeting up – either at my hotel or your place.

I am looking for a spanking session where you would play my naughty wife and me the cuckold husband. You would tease me about your lover and my own sexual inadequacies and receive a spanking on return – although I would be the one who would be the most humuliated!

Hope this is the sort of thing you might consider – I love your pics and promise that in all other respects apart from the obvious I am perfectly sane and normal!

Hope to hear from you soon.

F '

---oOo---

'Hi Lily-Rose,

Found your profile on Spankee****** and I would be interested in meeting you for a mild spanking session. Do you have a number I can call you on, please?

Also, do you have any more photos, please?

Looking forward to hearing from you.

SJ x '

---oOo---

The first two quoted above turned out to be too far away for either party to think it worthwhile.

The last of these three turned out to be only interested in my photos. I made the mistake of sending him two more photos. Over the six years since then, even after I gave up the spanking scene, he's contacted me numerous times, still asking for more photos (which I don't send) and still appears not to have any intention of meeting up.

Some just wanted to know what I would charge, where I operated, and whether I 'switched'. Switched? What did that mean, I wondered? I guessed that it meant switching positions from say, over a table, to over a bed. Yes, I thought I could manage that.

It turned out that 'switching' is where the spankee spanks the spanker. I considered this, but soon realised that it didn't interest me at all. About a quarter of all my replies were from people wanting to switch, so I had to turn them down. The idea of having to deal with a man bent over the bed, with his hairy buttocks and testicles on display, was an instant turn-off to me. I never felt the need or desire to dominate someone else, either verbally or physically.

It was scary and, at the same time, exciting to receive these replies. I didn't know if I would have the nerve to actually meet any of these guys. It felt so like prostitution. But at the same time, there should be no sex involved. I had to admit that I did like the idea of being spanked by a strange man, and the money made the whole idea very attractive. I wouldn't be doing it without the money, I decided. I would feel too cheap and desperate, strangely enough, without the excuse of the money to justify why I would take part in and probably enjoy such an activity.

*****

One sixty-five-year-old man contacted me, then once I replied, asked to meet up, so I gave him my mobile, still not sure by that time that I would be courageous enough to meet anyone face to face. He rang immediately and we started chatting. But after a few minutes I noticed that his voice was becoming slightly breathless. I had an inkling of what was going on. He suddenly said, 'I want you to treat me like a naughty schoolboy. You are my school headmistress and you are about to cane me.'

No thanks. This was not what I wanted. If this was the only type of caller, I wouldn't be pursuing this new career at all.

'Go on,' he pleaded, 'just say a few words.'

I suddenly felt sorry for him and said, very unconvincingly, 'You're a very naughty boy. Bend over my desk.' I heard this quiet exhalation of breath and he just said, 'That's it. I've come. Thank you.'

'You're welcome,' I said, and quickly put the phone down. I felt rather disgusted, even though I had chosen to take part. I wouldn't give out my mobile so readily next time.

*****

During the first few days after my website went live, when I had still not been brave enough to meet up with a client, a guy in his fifties contacted me. The below email has been quoted verbatim, apart from disguised names:

'Dear Lily-Rose,

I would be pleased to here more about your spanking services. I am a professional white gentleman in my early 50's who is an experienced spankee. My interests are purely pleasure related and I have no interest in, or any desire to hurt my spankee's. I particularly enjoy playing with an older lady and one who has other interests around which we could perhaps creat some interesting role-play scenarios.

If you are interested in playing you will find me to be reliable, discrete and good fun. I am based near Birmingham and can travel to suit you. I look forward to hearing from you

Joseph Joseph'

---oOo---

He was referring to the badminton and tennis on my website when he mentioned 'other interests'. I replied in the same polite vein:

'Hi Joseph,
Thanks very much for your reply. You sound like just the sort of spanker I would enjoy being spanked by.

I would do any role-play you would like. I may not have the clothes to begin with, but could probably build on that.

I am also reliable and discreet. This is, as you say, just a fun session for both of us.

We would have to talk on the phone first (5-10 mins), if it's OK with you.

My rates are £100 for the first hour, and £50 per hour after that (pro-rata).

I am about an hour south of Birmingham so we could meet half way, or I could come to your house.

I would prefer to go for a quick coffee/drink (10 mins) before following you back to the house/hotel.

If this sounds all OK so far, I can give you my mobile number.
Regards,
Lily-Rose'

---oOo---

His reply was equally as friendly and positive:

'Hi Lily-Rose,
Very happy with all that you suggest and agree that a coffee and a chat before a session would be sensible.

Do I take it that you are in the Chorton Common area? In which case it would be easy for me to make my way over to you and book a hotel room and take things from there.

I would be delighted to have a quick chat over te phone so please feel free to exchange numbers and I will call you at a suitable and agreed time
Kindest regards, Joseph'

It was a promising start to my first live encounter – but our session didn't pan out in the way either of us had envisaged. We had a brief conversation on the phone to discuss the details of meeting up for a coffee before getting down to business, and I detected an unkind, bullying tone, but I assumed this was normal for a spanker talking to a spankee. After the phone call, I realised I hadn't a clue what I should wear, and emailed him this question. (I also realised that I hadn't a clue what to say, how to behave or how to present myself for spanking.)

'I would be happy for you to wear similar knickers [to the website] but they won't be staying on for long!', he replied. 'For this to work for me I have to find you attractive and you need to excite me. The pictures I have seen certainly do that and I like what I learned about you over the telephone. Are you brave enough to send me more pictures to whet my appetite? I want to see one of your face and of you dressed.'

This all felt like the pre-cursor to a purely sexual encounter. I was beginning to realise how much spanking and sex were interlinked. With mounting trepidation, tinged with misgivings and excitement, I sent him the three photos I had used on dating sites.

'That's good. You have a good figure and I am looking forward to playing with you. You will be going naked with me and spanked very hard which will wipe that smile off your face. Do you understand?'

I realised that the mock bullying was all part of the lead-up to the spanking session, where he was obviously going to be the dominant one. But I wasn't sure about the naked part at all. *'I didn't agree to going naked so I might not do that,'* I replied. He backtracked hurriedly.

'Naked in terms of knickers down and shamefully round your ankles, legs apart and bent over a chair or the hotel bed ready to take a firm hand spanking and slippering. That is what I meant by you being naked.'

Good god. Would I be brave enough to go ahead with this, with a complete stranger? It became apparent that this very exchange was exciting him, and working up his appetite for the session. I was to find out that these initial emails and texts between spanker and spankee played a fairly important part in the overall sexiness and enjoyment of spanking sessions. Both parties finding out what the other liked, what positions and implements they preferred, and how far each was prepared to go. I was also surprised to learn just how much the spanker wants the spankee to be excited by the prospect of the session as well, for mutual enjoyment.

We arranged to meet at a pub so that I could feel safe with him. A huge, athletic-looking man of about six foot three met me in the car park. He seemed 'normal' and spoke with a very educated accent, so I decided I would at least have a drink with him. It felt weird to be having a drink with a guy who was soon going to be taking my knickers down and spanking my bare bottom, having only just met me. He told me that he'd been with his previous spankee for years, and that unfortunately she'd had to move away. As he talked, I realised he was in love with her. That was a revelation in itself. I thought men would consider spankees as inferior prostitutes, not equals with whom they could fall in love.

He also made it clear that he thought it patronising of me on my website to state that I would not perform sexual favours, or take drugs, as in his opinion it suggested that spankers would all take drugs and automatically ask for sex, and were unaware of the unwritten rules surrounding spanking sites. He also said it looked as if I thought I was sexually attractive to all men. I didn't agree with him at all, especially as Duncan himself had suggested disclaiming sexual favours, but I was keen to avoid an argument with my first spanker before we had even started the session, so I said only, 'Hmmm – maybe.' (However, looking back over the eighteen months, I realise I never encountered any spanker that even hinted at taking drugs, either with or without me, so it seems Joseph was right about the drugs part. When I set up the website, of course, I thought it was a lowlife world, full of junkies.)

After this slightly awkward drink, we decided to walk over to the nearby Travelodge, where he had booked a room for the afternoon. Privately I was beginning to realise he was not someone I would find endearing in normal life. That short walk was a journey into the unknown. Potentially dangerous, potentially painful, definitely intriguing and full of trepidation for me, whereas he seemed to be taking it all in his very long stride. As we walked past my car, I realised I could simply get in and drive away, but I was committed by then. I was going to see it through.

As soon as we were inside the room, his personality changed.

'Stand over there,' he barked, pointing to a spot near the bed.

I did as I was told, feeling nervous and excited at the same time. He took off his jacket and handed it to me.

'Hang this up!'

I took it from him, but instead of hanging it up, I decided to give him an excuse to spank me, so I threw it onto the bed behind him, where it lay in a crumpled heap. He stared at me in surprise. Instead of grabbing me and putting me over his knee, as I had envisaged, he just turned round and picked up his jacket and hung it up on a hanger himself, looking slightly nonplussed. I later learnt that most dominants just want their spankees to do as they're told. They will engineer the reason for a spanking from a huge variety of make-believe punishment scenarios. They certainly don't need a spankee to try and be 'naughty' from the current real-life situation.

He came over and stood right next to me at right angles to my body and grabbed my arm. His six foot three towered over my five foot three. I wasn't sure whether to look him in the eye, so decided not to.

'Stand up straight!' he ordered. I did so. Without hesitation, he bent over me and started to spank me hard over my jeans for a few minutes. It stung, but it was easily bearable at this point. There had been no warm-up slaps. I made no noise during this initial spanking. I wasn't sure whether I was supposed to either.

Without asking, he pulled my jeans down to my knees. It felt weird that I was still standing up. And how vulnerable I felt in the grip of this huge stranger. He slapped me hard on the buttocks with his enormous hand ten or twelve times. This time it stung a lot, but I still let out no cry. He pushed my shoulders very slightly forward to encourage me to stick my bottom out. Then he roughly pulled my knickers down to my knees and continued the hand spanking. Another ten or so slaps reigned down.

'Can I see your breasts?' he asked.

'No,' I answered.

There was a slight pause. 'Then take off your knickers and jeans.'

I took them off where I stood, and as I bent right over to finally jerk the jeans from my feet, I was almost bent double in front of him.

'Stay in that position,' he commanded. Then he spanked me hard again for about five minutes.

'Right. Stand up and bend over the bed with your feet apart.'

I started coming out of myself and watching myself going through the motions. I was way out of my comfort zone and couldn't really believe that I was going through with this. I knew I could probably just say that I couldn't do it anymore, and I was pretty certain that he would let me go. But I needed the money, and really it was such easy money. It was just fleeting pain to be endured for a minute or two, after all.

I bent slightly over the bed with my hands spread in front of me, and placed my feet about a foot apart. He took a chair, placed it directly behind me and sat down. I could feel his eyes on my body.

'Feet wider apart,' he ordered. 'I would like to see more of that extremely wet pussy.' It was true that despite my misgivings about launching headlong into unchartered territory, I was incredibly turned on by the proceedings.

'No,' I said defiantly.

'OK,' he said, eventually. 'Turn around and put yourself over my knee.'

I could do that, I thought, although my bottom was beginning to feel beleaguered. I placed myself over his knee, and to my surprise he started caressing my bottom gently, and chatting to me again, as if we were old friends. After about five minutes of this, he asked what I felt like doing.

'Well, I've got a slipper if you want to try that,' I said. He agreed and I naively took out of my bag a man's heavy, ribbed slipper, which I had bought that day. He grabbed it eagerly, commanded me to stand up, and, bending over me again, walloped me with it hard about ten times. It certainly hurt – but I just stood there and took it, thinking this must be normal.

Suddenly he stopped abruptly. He stood upright, took a look at my buttocks and said 'I can't use this bottom. It bruises far too easily. I think you've had enough.'

He gave me back my slipper. I felt quite disappointed that I seemed to have failed as a fledgling spankee.

'How much do I owe you?' he asked, rather gruffly.

'£100 is fine.'

'Here's £120 – for the petrol.' He handed me a wadge of £20 notes.

'I won't count them,' I said to him, slightly embarrassed at being paid for our interaction and trying to show that I trusted him. This seemed to infuriate him.

'Well I counted them out in front of you,' he snapped. I mumbled that I hadn't been watching him count it out, but the atmosphere had changed, and he was clearly annoyed. He was probably also disappointed at the session and my lack of willingness to reveal all. Then, bizarrely, he suddenly took me in his arms and started caressing my head. I came up to his chest. He could very easily have broken my neck with one little twist of his huge hands, but instinct told me that a guy who refused to carry on slippering me for humane reasons would probably not then want to kill me.

'You OK, small person?' he asked gently.

I assured him I was, and then decided to put my arms round his waist, which made the situation even more weird and embarrassing.

'You don't have to do that,' he said, and extricated himself from my grip. Then he thanked me, told me not to ring his mobile because of his wife, and left quickly.

Phew! I'd survived my first spanking session. My bottom was smarting. I hadn't really enjoyed it and I hadn't liked the guy very much. He was a bully, and impatient, even out of spanker-domination mode.

I walked over to the mirror and turned my back to it. My bottom was very red, and was flecked with tiny blue bruises all over. The next day when I surveyed the damage, it was a mess. Not only was it covered in small black, blue and purple bruises, but two slipper-shaped marks were magnificently apparent.

I was unashamedly proud of having taken such punishment with no complaints. I took several photos of my rear with the slipper held next to it to compare bruise mark sizes and shapes.

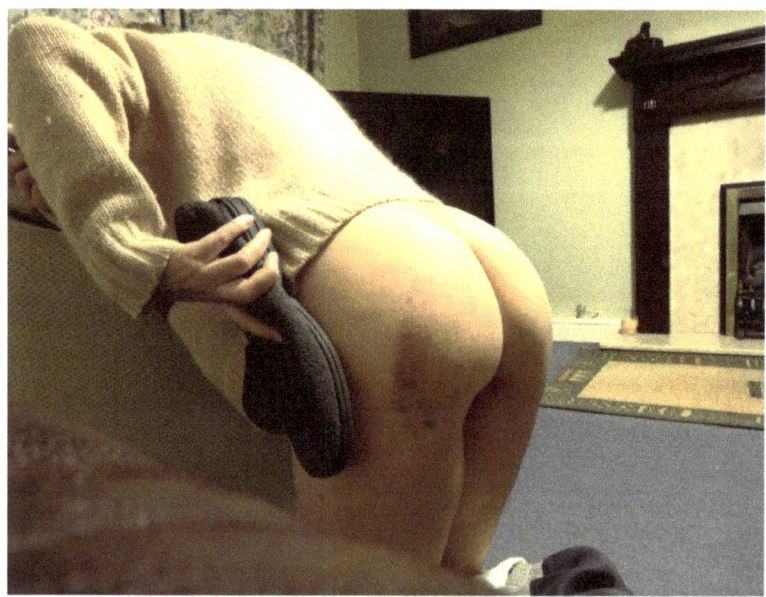

My first spanking, and, as it turned out, slippering left my bottom fairly bruised. Note that the shape of the bruise matches that of the slipper.

I was about to send the best one to him when I saw that he'd sent an email.

'*Hi – how are you and that gorgeous bottom of yours?*'

I was surprised he cared or bothered to get in touch again after what I considered must have been a fairly disappointing session.

'*Strange to get an email from someone who's just thrashed the shit out of me, asking about my welfare,*' I joked in reply. '*Here's a photo of your handiwork.*'

He didn't seem amused. '*I didn't thrash the shit out of you. I like to spank hard, that's all. Thanks for the photo. I've seen worse. It reminds me of what a nice little body you have.*'

'*Thanks for the extra £20. Sorry I was so wilful – that was just play-acting, so you could have something to spank me for, but that obviously wasn't what you wanted. And I hope I didn't crease your jacket. So if we do meet again, I will just be subservient.*'

'*Not a problem. It's always a challenge to deal with my subs' different behaviours. Thank you for your note. I hope your bottom is still stinging but that the marks and reddening are reducing. You have a delicate bottom that you will need to be careful with.*

Anyway it was a pleasure to meet you and if you enjoyed yourself I hope that we may be able to do it again sometime.

Kindest regards
Joseph'

---oOo---

I assumed that by 'subs' he meant submissives. I quite liked the idea of being a submissive within a spanking context, although I wasn't sure the verbal bullying when the spanking had finished was acceptable, but perhaps that was all part of the scene.

He didn't ask for another session. I assumed it was a combination of the fact that my bottom couldn't take his strength of spanking, that I refused to undress and that we hadn't got along that well as people, however polite his emails seemed.

Interesting though. That first encounter had demonstrated two things to me: that it was much more of a social interaction than a financial agreement, and that spankers can care about their 'subs' and need them to be engaged in the session, and equally excited by it, for the session to work for the spanker.

I later learnt that the spanking world didn't like terms such as 'beat' and 'hit' as that sounded non-consensual and abusive. 'Spank', 'strap', 'thrash', and 'smack' were much preferred, as these words denoted punishment, the premise behind every CP interaction. Also frowned on were terms such as 'arse', 'bum', 'butt' and 'backside'. They are seen as crass, with no decorum. 'Bottom' was easily preferred to anything else, although occasionally I heard people say 'behind', 'seat' and 'derriere'.

Hence Joseph's dislike of my 'accusing' him of having 'thrashed the shit' out of me, even if I had been joking.

About a year later, when I'd become much more familiar with expected spankee behaviour, and had been taking fairly hard hand-spankings, strappings, crop thrashings, beltings and some canings, I contacted him again, partly to make amends for my earlier failure. I mentioned that I was quite happy to go completely naked with him this time.

He agreed to another session, and we arranged the place and time for the next day. Then I emailed him to request that he desist from verbally bullying me as much as last time, when not 'playing'. He replied immediately to say he was taken aback that I thought he had bullied me outside of play, and that it was unintentional.

The next day he wrote another email, saying that, coincidentally, his first spankee had suddenly returned to the area and that he would be taking things up with her again. A likely story. I never heard from him again.

Chapter 5

My Youngest Spanker

The third email I received through my web page ad was from a surprisingly young but experienced spanker, who had been a spankee himself.

'Hi Lily-Rose, lovely pictures, you have a gorgeous bottom. Mid 20's, fit athletic chap here, especially like spanking the more mature lady, just wandering on your rates? - Paul.'

As a student he couldn't afford my usual price of £100 an hour so we negotiated a reduced rate of £40 for half an hour. I needed all the money and experience I could acquire. It's entirely up to the spanker and spankee involved to make a financial arrangement and stick to it. It's almost a case of 'my word is my bond' (or should that be bondage). I didn't come across any spanker who either tried not to pay or attempted to change the rate once agreed. This young guy did, however, say he had once allowed himself to be spanked by someone who had then left without paying, so he warned me to be on the alert.

We met for a quick drink at a Travelodge, where he had booked a room. I always insisted on this pre-spanking initial assessment time if I hadn't met the guy before. He seemed a nice young man; fairly shy but polite and respectful, with none of the bullying tendencies of the first guy. After only about ten minutes, we both decided we had finished talking, and it would be safe to start the spanking session, so we went straight up to the room.

I wondered if my being old enough to be his mother, and his rather endearing lack of confidence, would make him hesitate to start actually spanking me. Not a chance. He wasted no time in putting me over his knee, fully dressed in my skimpy, khaki short summer dress, where he proceeded to give me a gentle hand spanking to warm me up. Being warmed up makes a big difference to how much punishment you can take later in the session. It's also a nice, kind gesture to do for your fellow player. Soon my dress came up and my knickers came down and a harder hand spanking ensued, for a solid five minutes or so.

'Take your knickers off and put yourself in the wheelbarrow position,' he suddenly said.

'What's that?'

'OK. Lie on your front on my thighs with each leg either side of my body. Your hands on the floor. Your bottom facing me and the ceiling.'

OMG. How personal is that going to be?

I managed with some difficulty to place myself across him, in the requested position, feeling slightly self-conscious that such a young man could now peruse every crevice I owned. As he started to spank my buttocks again, he remarked with a laugh that it was a 'nice view'. He never touched me anywhere other than my bottom. It might have been strange to have such young fingers feel my body but I decided I would have let him had he asked. The half-hour extended to an hour, but he was such a gentleman and we got on so well as people that I didn't mind at all. I could have left at any time if I had wanted. I accepted the £40 as agreed.

*****

A few months later, Paul got in touch again. He said he was in the area and would I like to have another session at the same price as before. He asked if it could be outside this time. At this point in my eighteen-month period as a spankee, I had tried a few outside sessions and had found out that it's actually quite difficult to find a suitable location in this crowded little island of ours that is hidden, comfortable, suitable for bending over, and far enough away from humanity for the slaps, strokes, beltings and yelps to be inaudible to the local population.

I live near a petrol station so we met there in our respective cars. I headed out towards a little nearby village, with this young spanker following in his car in close, eager pursuit. I stopped outside a church, and he got out to discuss our next, clandestine move. It was dusk, and there was no one about, but there were a few houses dotted along the road near the church, and we imagined unseen eyes watching our illicit activity. While not actually wanting to be seen or caught in the act, the thought that it could possibly happen rather added to the excitement. We started to giggle and laugh. I didn't know if a bare-bottomed spanking outside was against the law, but I suspected that a by-law against gross indecency, a breach of the peace or performing a lewd act in public probably existed for this sort of activity.

We looked around at the surrounding fields for a suitable log or fence for me to bend over, but they were all too exposed. We were about to try somewhere else when I noticed the church had a fair covering of trees and bushes in its graveyard. Would it be illegal to carry out a bare-bottomed spanking within church grounds? We weren't sure. We walked up the churchyard path and tried the church door, which was locked, suggesting no service was taking place and no clergy in the vicinity. But after a few hurried whispered discussions, we decided spanking within a graveyard would be too disrespectful and probably sacrilegious.

We walked round to the back of the church. Directly behind the church was a small field. Close to the fence that separated the graveyard from the field was a magnificent tree, with a bough that extended out at my waist height. We had found the ideal site. Looking quickly around, we clambered over the fence and approached our friend the tree that was to harbour and witness a slightly different activity than its neighbour the church normally hosted.

Paul indicated that I should bend over the bough. As I did so, I felt him approach me and stand silently behind me in the half-light. He started spanking me lightly over my dress for a few minutes. Then the dress was pulled up, my knickers were quickly pulled down to my ankles, and he continued spanking me slightly harder. After a while, he suggested I undress completely. I considered the possibility of a vicar suddenly appearing from behind the trunk of the tree and wondered what excuse we would conjure up for being naked in a field next to his graveyard. But it was too sexy a moment to miss; undressing in the middle of a tree on the edge of a field next to a churchyard in near darkness in front of a man I had only met once before. Once completely naked, I bent over the bough again.

I expected the hand-spanking to continue but then heard the unbuckling of his belt. 'Are you OK with this?' I assured him I was, as long as it wasn't too hard. I heard the swish of the belt through the air and it landed with a sting across both buttocks. I made a gasping noise. Seven or eight strokes followed, with a pause of a few seconds between each one. Paul was savouring the moment.

We started to wonder if the strokes and my gasps would be heard by someone, so we decided not to push our luck. As Paul stood guard, looking out for disconsolate priests, I began to get dressed. Just as I was pulling my dress on, Paul suddenly whispered, 'Shh. Someone's coming.' He had spotted a jogger heading in our direction. The man luckily seemed completely focused on his running and never looked in our direction. He passed within twenty yards of us but seemed oblivious to my increasingly hurried movements.

'That was close,' Paul remarked. We started to chuckle that we had got away with such outrageous activity. It was a spanking session that neither of us would ever forget. Here's to trees with low boughs and absent vicars.

Chapter 6

Why Spanking?

As the emails increased, I started to wonder why people wanted to spank or be spanked. Did it always start with a spanking or caning as a child? My initial thoughts were that this is not the origin because such activity was not associated with enjoyment or titillation by the child, even if it was by some of the perpetrators. And it definitely wasn't associated with sex by most children. Punishment certainly. But not sexy punishment. On the other hand, most of the spankers I met were middle-class and in their late fifties and early sixties, so a good proportion of them could have been to schools that advocated the cane. Even if a caning was not enjoyed at the time, it might have sewn an unconscious seed for punishment later on in life in a controlled and fun scenario. Caning certainly seemed to feature as a highly prised activity by many spankers.

I asked a few of the spankers why they wanted to spank. No one knew. They only knew they had had the desire to spank for many years but not dared tell anyone, especially their partners. The internet had, for some, opened up the world of spanking in a delightful and convenient way. It had been such a relief, they told me, to meet fellow spankers and chat about their secret fetish.

One guy told me he felt he had been 'let out of solitary confinement.'

Another guy, who sometimes organised spanking parties, told me, 'I had a nice lunch today with a couple of former work colleagues. The only drawback is that there is only so far talk of decorating and gardening will take one, before starting to sound boring. But I have to sit there quietly, suppressing all the things I'd really like to talk about, like my latest party or the exciting blonde who travelled halfway across the country just to have her bottom spanked.'

Growing up, I had hardly been subjected to corporal punishment at all. My parents usually had only to resort to a quiet 'Steady' if any of us three girls crossed the line, and we would know we had gone too far. When my older sister, Grace, was six and I was four, she decided it would be a good idea to start hitting me with a metal clothes hanger, so I found one of my own and started hitting her back. Mum heard the commotion, marched into the bedroom and put Grace over her knee for a spanking. I had to watch, knowing that the same fate awaited me. And it duly came, while I protested my innocence. I still remember my outrage at the miscarriage of justice. It was self-defence. That was the only spanking I ever received from either of my parents.

My father never laid a finger on us in anger or for discipline. When I was eight, Mum gave the back of my hand one light slap for being cheeky. I was furious that she could assault me like that. One other time she gave me one slap on the bottom for the same reason, as I stood naked in the bathroom in front of her. I felt humiliated, especially since one of my sisters was around and I imagined her being secretly pleased to have witnessed it.

Those three incidents, though, have remained clear in my memory, so you could argue that a measured slap does have the desired effect of letting the child know they have gone too far, whereas I must have received hundreds of verbal reprimands from both parents and can't remember any one of them specifically (except when my mother caught me kissing my boyfriend, who had his hand up my blouse in the front of his car on my parents' drive when I was fifteen). I don't look back on those three events with a fond chuckle even now. Surprisingly, I still regard them as an impertinence, and an unnecessary use of force, however gently and lovingly administered. In my mind, they were an assault, a betrayal.

I certainly didn't enjoy them in any way.

At school, there was no corporate punishment either. I remember our PE teacher, who we had all decided was a lesbian without really knowing what that entailed, once being so tired of our class's misbehaviour during a netball lesson that she suddenly shouted at us all, 'If you lot don't stop messing around, you will feel the weight of my hand.'

We weren't quite sure what 'feel the weight' meant, but were convinced it had something to do with her being a lesbian and wanting to slap our faces or bottoms with her hand. We also knew it was a completely empty threat as physical punishment didn't feature in such a nice 'High School for Girls'.

Although corporate punishment was not heard of at school, that didn't stop one of my friends and I, at the age of eleven, devising reasons to spank each other over the playground wall behind a cluster of bushes. We would conjure up an extremely fragile excuse that the other person needed to be punished; she would bend over the wall, her skirt taken up, and three or four very light slaps would be administered over her knickers. That was until one day the playground duty teacher decided to include the space behind the bushes as part of her round, and found one of us bent over the wall with our skirt up. She very politely asked us to desist in this activity, which we did immediately and hurriedly, and we never heard anything from her again. We guessed that she might have been too embarrassed to raise the subject with the headmistress and thought it wise just to let it drop.

I have no idea why we wanted to take part in this activity. We weren't lesbians, and we were too young to equate these little slaps with sex. I don't remember ever wishing during these sessions that my female friend was a boy. By the age of fourteen, things had changed. For a start, we no longer played or wanted to play these childish games with each other. Hormones had kicked in, and sexual maturity had made me wake up to the existence of boys, and to films in which men like John Wayne and Elvis Presley were seen spanking women, who were shrieking and kicking in mock protest. Scenes like these seeped into my imagination as a young girl, and I would dream about being spanked myself by some tall, strong man. This would be somebody in authority, or quite often a man who I imagined was my somewhat older boyfriend at the time. I would be taken suddenly over the knee and it would always be for some misdemeanour. The spanking would only last a few seconds, not the many minutes that I experienced later as a spankee (ten continuous minutes with no rubs was the longest spanking given to me by a particularly zealous spanker). In my imagined scenarios, it would always be given with affection, and with a view to improving my behaviour, never with harmful or abusive intent.

But why? Why would I imagine scenes in which men would have to punish me when my only relevant experience as a child had left me enraged, indignant and frustrated?

I was quite a naïve teenager. I had only girls at home, apart from an uncommunicative and undemonstrative father, with whom I had little in common. I had only girls in the neighbourhood to play with, apart from two little boys next door who were younger than me, and who disappeared off to boarding school at the age of eleven. There were only girls at school. I lived in a female-dominated world, where I flourished. I did have a boyfriend from the age of fifteen to eighteen, but somehow I knew him so well and he was such a kind, gentle chap that it didn't seem to prepare me for a world of men.

When I was fourteen, I persuaded my mother to let me go by myself to the local youth club, unaware of the sort of streetwise kids that frequented it. I walked into the rather decrepit hall and noticed a group of teenage boys and girls standing around at the other end. They looked up quickly but didn't say anything, and carried on chatting amongst themselves in the local accent. I didn't know what to do, so stood against the wall, feeling self-conscious and awkward.

After a few minutes, a boy of about fifteen approached me, and said simply, 'How are you doing?'

I went into a panic. 'Shut up,' was all I could come up with. He patted me on the head and actually said, 'Keep taking the pills,' before walking away and joining his friends on the other side of the hall, where he no doubt told them I was a posh idiot. I was mortified and left straight away, vowing never to try and find a boyfriend outside my normal circles.

On leaving school at eighteen, I was woefully ill-prepared for a world where men would often be my managers, colleagues, sports teammates, or simply present in my social circles. At that time, I all but viewed men as an alien species, with whom I couldn't be myself, and whom I felt I had to impress all the time.

In my twenties and thirties I was sexually very attracted to men – all kinds of men, although stupidly I would prefer the tall, muscly, athletic types. If I could only now tell my young self that it's often the short, weedier ones that are the nicest. I would always be aware of a good-looking guy and try and catch his attention. I was very pretty, sporty and petite, so I found it easy to attract first dates, but often they would tire of my lack of confidence and inability to talk naturally to them, and not feel they were getting to know the real me.

It probably took me until my mid-thirties before I could talk authentically to a man, and behave just like I behaved with my female friends. What a waste of effort for all those years to have tried so hard to be something I wasn't. This is apparently quite common among pupils of single-sex schools, exacerbated by having only their own sex siblings at home. It can cause untold misery for years and indeed a life-changing inability to find a suitable partner and/or keep long-term relationships.

I watched my niece and nephew, who grew up with each other, and were educated in a comprehensive school, behave totally naturally around friends of the opposite sex. My current partner and I watch with envy as his son in his early twenties doesn't change an iota of his character around the many girls in his social circle.

Was this immature, unrealistic attitude of mine towards men partly responsible for my desire to be spanked by them? Why would

I not want a boyfriend to be just a friend and lover, rather than some authoritative power controlling me with occasional corporate punishment?

Sometimes with boyfriends, I would try and initiate a spanking from them. I would do something slightly naughty and occasionally they would give me a playful slap. But, of course, I wanted a harder, longer spanking. I would do the naughty thing again, but it would mostly result in the guy just getting slightly irritated, which almost always meant no repeat spanking. Paradoxically, if you are actually annoyed by someone, you don't normally want to spank them. Spanking is for sexy fun, not as a result of their getting on your nerves. I quickly abandoned this goal and relegated it to the unrequited fetish quarter of my brain.

The more I thought about the origins and reasons for so many people wanting to spank, the more I came to the conclusion that sex is the most important factor in spanking. Bottoms are an integral part of finding a member of the opposite sex attractive. If a man tries to give a woman a playful slap, she pretty much knows he finds her attractive.

Having come off HRT recently, my bottom has lost some of its firm pertness and I've realised that I now feel less interested in being spanked as I don't feel as sexually attractive.

If a man puts his hand on a woman's bottom, it suggests ownership or intended ownership in some way, however un-PC that sounds. Either he is her sexual partner already, or he would like to be. A man would not put his hand on the bottom of another man's wife. The bottom is so close to the sexual organs, inviting vaginal or anal sexual entry between the buttocks, that it's one small step for man to go from spanking to imagining, or taking part in, any number of sexual acts.

And, paradoxically, the bottom plays absolutely no physical part in conception. It's only function within the body seems to be to allow us to sit down, or, arguably, to protect the anus. Why would it hold so much fascination for many men and women? And why would slapping it, instead of caressing it, be deemed so sexy?

I've heard it said that a spanking sometimes vibrates the clitoris, which is then stimulated. That might explain some of the excitement surrounding spankings, but there's a whole domination/submissive power struggle going on between the sexes during a spanking, which is way more psychological and intriguing than the mechanical stimulation of a tiny clitoris, even if men this time conveniently don't have to try and find it.

In *The Naked Ape,* Desmond Morris describes how we are arguably the sexiest species on earth. Unlike most other species, we have regular sex just for the sake of it, not just for procreation. The human female body has features accentuated for sex rather than reproduction. For example, the shape of the breasts emulates that of the bottom, even though the very fullness of the breast makes it harder for infants to suckle the nipple. In other primates, the nipple is long and thin, making it easier for infants to attach themselves. Our mouth lips, exacerbated by lipstick, reflect our vaginal lips.

If I imagine a woman spanking me, it holds no attraction at all. If a skinny little guy of 4'6" tried to spank me, unfortunately, that wouldn't be sexy for me either. I can only imagine that it has something to do with the law of the jungle, which is mostly unspoken in our unnatural world. Female animals often look for a strong, dominant male in a partner for procreation and protection. Are we so far from that animalistic instinct?

A strong male also denotes health, which suggests fertility, which is the cornerstone to male attractiveness in nature but also in the human world, albeit subliminally. A pert female bottom suggests youth, fitness, health, muscular strength and fertility. A flabby bottom might suggest weakness, lack of fitness, old age and possibly ill-health and infertility.

Maybe it's because we do live in such an unnatural world that we women secretly yearn for some permitted male-domination that is only associated with the physical difference between a man and woman, a difference that we have little control over. Hence the popularity of the *'Fifty Shades'* trilogy. It should be noted that many women didn't want to acknowledge that they had bought all three books, as if they were ashamed to admit that they were interested in spanking, or in the idea of being spanked, I imagine for fear of being seen as weak, childish, or having a secret fetish.

The fact that many women want a hard, 'proper' spanking is also a strange but very real phenomenon. Why would we want pain, and, believe me, spankings can hurt, even given with a hand. I imagine that if a spanking is so gentle that it doesn't cause pain, it could be perceived that the perpetrator is weak, or is too afraid to show real discipline. And who wants a weak spanker, would be the cry?

A school friend once confided in me in our early twenties that she wouldn't respect a man until he had spanked her. She, too, had only female siblings at home and had gone to the same single-sex school as me. In her eyes, the spanking had to be for a misdemeanour, and fairly hard. The man had to be annoyed enough to administer a 'proper' spanking, rather than a contrived, flirty spanking. Apparently, an American boyfriend did spank her some time later for some wrongdoing and that sealed the relationship for her.

I was sometimes asked if I felt humiliated as I lay over someone's knee with knickers down, or over some piece of furniture, perhaps stripped naked from the waist down, with legs apart. This question would be asked both within role-play and outside it. The answer would always be 'no'. Spankers just always seemed to be genuinely grateful that I would share such a spankable bottom with them, which made me feel almost benevolent and generous, and in no way humiliated. Within role-play, if they stated they wanted me to feel humiliated as part of the punishment, I would refuse to admit anything approaching humiliation, partly to give them an added excuse to continue the punishment.

But however much a woman might enjoy a spanking, if a man nowadays tries to dominate her mentally, bully her verbally or patronise her, the average intelligent woman in the Western world won't find it acceptable or amusing or flirty in any way. He will normally be told in no uncertain terms that that sort of behaviour is intolerable. Ten minutes later he might be allowed to spank her over his knee with knickers down. No wonder men are confused.

Chapter 7

Party-Lover Jeremy

Soon after my website went live, I received another very polite email from a 62-year-old man called Jeremy:

'Hello Lily-Rose,
This is Jeremy from Chasenell. I am an experienced player and have been active in both the party and 121 scene for about 10 years. I've just seen your profile on the website. As a newcomer, I expect that you are inundated with enquiries, but in due course I would be very interested in meeting you for a 121. So if you'd like to, do please get back to me when you have the chance.
All the best for now, Jeremy. '

I liked the sound of him and the fact that he was experienced, so I emailed back straight away. I wasn't quite sure of some of the terms he'd used but, from the tone of his email, I felt that he wouldn't mind explaining them to me since I was a novice.

'Hi Jeremy,
Thanks very much for your email. I've had several enquiries but I'm certainly not inundated. I imagine the age does not help. What is a 121? I assume it's one woman with two men? I would only try that after I had met you once or maybe twice. My rates are £100 for the first hour, and £50 per hour after that. Would you prefer to meet in a hotel/lodge or your house?
Regards,
Lily-Rose '

As predicted, I received a kind explanatory email by return:

'Dear Lily-Rose,

Thanks for getting back to me. It's true I suppose that most of the girls in the 'scene' (as we often refer to it), are somewhat younger. But nevertheless there are still a number of very attractive spankees of various levels of experience who are in their 40s and 50s. Although age might be a factor in the level of response you are getting, on the other hand, your profile on the whole is highly attractive.

The term 121 is a very confusing 'text-style' abbreviation of the phrase 'one-to-one', meaning 'one-on-one' or one man/one woman. (Other numerical combinations like 221 or 122 are of course also possible, but quite rare.) A 'party' has multiple players of both genders, normally in a ratio of between 2 or 3 men to each woman. But don't worry, I'm just enquiring about a straightforward 'one on one' meeting. I would prefer to meet at my home, where I live alone. Before arranging a meeting, however, I would appreciate the opportunity of having a brief telephone conversation with you.

Best regards, Jeremy.'

We had a brief but very cordial phone conversation, in which he was just as pleasant and kind as his emails suggested. We arranged that I would spend an afternoon and probably an evening with him in his house, since it was one and half hours away. He assured me he would pay me for the petrol. He said he had a playroom, which I was very eager to see – but not necessarily try out. I had read *Fifty Shades of Grey* and imagined it would be decked out with chains, whips and whipping benches.

I arrived at the appointed time and knocked on the door of a big, detached Victorian house in a very well-to-do residential area. A slim, clean-shaven man with short, dark hair, dressed in smart-casuals, opened the door. Smiling, he greeted me with a hug.

'Come in and have a cup of tea,' he said, taking my coat. He led the way into his conservatory, which looked out onto his lovely garden. 'Would you like some biscuits?'

We sat and had afternoon tea, chatting as usual in these situations about our spanking experiences. Through the conservatory windows, I could see a bowling green, where people in white were playing bowls yards from a garden that probably held many a salacious secret. Little did they know what was about to happen here in this house that afternoon, and what, it transpired, frequently happened in fairly large numbers, behind closed doors here.

Jeremy and I discovered we were on the same dating site, which gave us two good subjects for discussion. He agreed how hard it was to find a partner who liked the spanking scene. (Non-spankers, both men and women, are described as 'vanilla'.) He told me he had once been on a few dates with a girl and then decided to tell her about his spanking interest. She was horrified, and he never saw her again.

I finished my tea and looked expectantly at him. Sometimes it was a little awkward finishing the social chit-chat at the beginning of a session and starting the spanking itself, especially when you didn't know each other very well.

'Right. Shall we get going?' he said. 'I think a little role-play would break the ice, don't you?'

'Yes, that's fine,' I said, trying to sound confident, but inside I was dreading having to do my first role-play. I had always avoided acting parts in plays at school. I was just too self-conscious.

'What would you like to play?' I asked. We had discussed by email different scenarios, and he had asked me to invent one. I was surprised that many spankers liked to take part in role-plays of the spankees' choice rather than their own. It means they know the spankee is more engaged in the interaction. They often reiterated how important it was to them that the spankee enjoy herself during the session.

He suddenly took on a serious demeanour. 'In a few minutes I want you to stand outside the playroom, and knock on the door,' he said. 'I will be inside behind the desk. Come and report yourself like we agreed.'

I waited for him to go into the room, then after a minute or so went along and knocked on the door, my heart thumping.

'Come,' he shouted.

As soon as I opened the door, a completely different character sat behind the desk, staring at me gravely. To my disappointment, the room had no whips, chains or whipping benches, although part of me was relieved. It was just an ordinary, carpeted, fairly small lounge, with a writing desk, two chairs, and a sideboard with a goldfish in a fishbowl.

'Come and stand in front of me,' he said sternly. 'Why have you been reported to me?'

I tried to tell my agreed story – that I'd been caught red-handed stealing apples in his orchard by a gardener and been ordered to report to him (the rich landowner), to be dealt with accordingly, or he would go to the police. But whenever my eyes met his, I was just aware that this was the guy I had just been having afternoon tea with five minutes before. I started to smile self-consciously, so I kept looking away, trying to concentrate on the scenario so that I could look contrite. Nerves were playing a part.

He kept up the solemn pretence of the role-play expertly, even in the face of my fading prowess as the leading lady.

'You have to choose between a severe spanking from me, or the police.'

I tried desperately to get into the part. 'But what's wrong with taking those apples? They were on the ground. No one would want them anyway.'

'You know very well that stealing my apples and trespassing on my land is a crime. Choose what your punishment is to be.'

Then my eyes met his, and I committed the mortal sin of laughing. I really didn't want to, and regretted it immediately, but I was too nervous to stop it. I wondered if he would be annoyed that I didn't seem to be taking this role-play seriously. I was annoyed with myself – he seemed a nice guy, and deserved to be treated with respect; moreover to get his money's worth from this spanking session, which would only be enhanced by a good initial role-play. I managed to say that I didn't want him to go to the police.

He cleverly and kindly rescued the situation. 'Right. I will wipe that smile off your face. Come and stand over here.' He got up and sat down on the chair in the middle of the room and pulled me roughly over his knee. He had even put a small stool for my elbows to rest on. I was sorry that I had almost ruined the moment, but he seemed to have forgiven me.

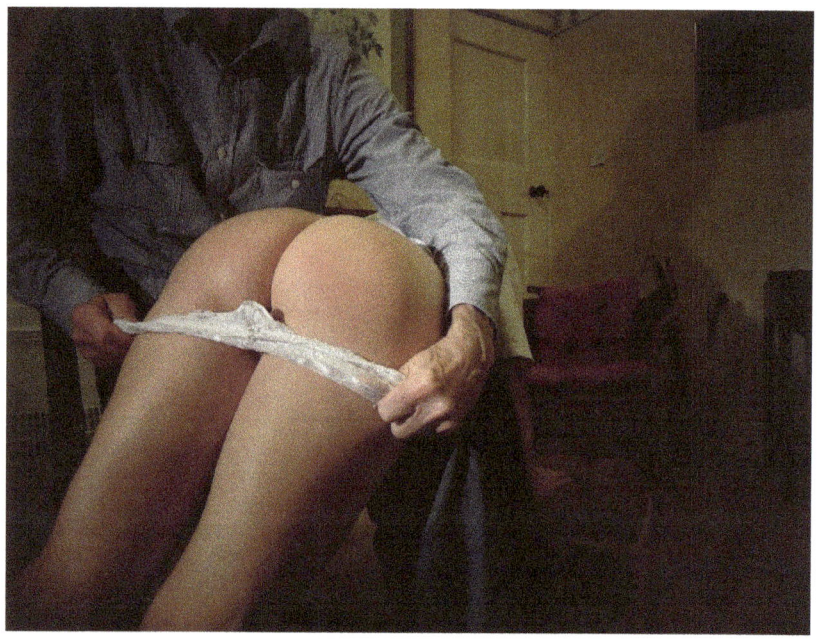

OTK with Jeremy. Note the variety of canes in the background, and the stool placed conveniently for my elbows and hands for comfort.

This photo was later shown to a spankee, aged 45, who had been worrying about her looks. She said she found my picture inspirational.

"If my bottom is a good as hers at 57, I'll have no worries."

I sent a message back to her to say that HRT helped.

Jeremy also emailed me recently and generously expressed praise for my bottom. *'I don't think you realised how good looking you were as a spankee – pity in a way that more people did not get to appreciate. Makes me feel quite privileged.'*

It was a great session, which I thoroughly enjoyed. I was spanked for the next two hours in various different positions, with knickers up as well as down. He was so experienced that he was used to dealing with novice spankees and tailored the whole session to my needs.

Initially, he warmed up my bottom with a gentle hand-spanking over his knee (OTK). Then, for variety, we tried several different pieces of furniture in his main lounge – over the desk, over the table and over the end of a chaise longue.

He had quite an array of implements, which I'd never seen before or tried, or even heard of. He tried them on me one by one, very gently to begin with, always asked for my permission first, and always stopped immediately if I asked him to. There were several types of strap (a thick, short leather belt), a paddle (a round malleable leather implement, shaped like a huge lollipop, which made a lovely loud thwack on my bottom, with not too much pain), a riding crop (which stung) and a flogger (a small cluster of light leathery thongs attached to a handle, which he applied to my back and which made a loud thud but was surprisingly more ticklish than painful, perhaps because he didn't apply much force). There were also several canes of different lengths and thicknesses, but I said I didn't think I was ready to try them out.

Throughout this first session with him, he never tried to touch me anywhere other than my bottom. My knickers did come off completely at one point and my legs were pushed apart over the desk. I looked round, and he was squatting down between my legs, having a good gawp. Fine by me. After the first spanker had asked to see my breasts and crotch, and I'd refused in a fit of defiance, I had decided that I might quite like men to look at me. I did, in fact, find this aspect of spanking sessions extremely erotic, as Jeremy could tell from the amount of lubrication oozing from me. It was actually dripping onto the floor, so much so that he kept having to hand me tissues, and at one point helped to dry me off.

'I'm glad you're enjoying yourself so much,' he chuckled. 'It's much nicer for me that I see you are so turned on by it. And by the way. it's disgraceful.'

I explained that I was on HRT, which helped the body lubricate. We agreed that perhaps I was on too high a dose.

The session ended, and we had another cup of tea. He wondered about taking me outside for another spanking session in his garden, but people were still playing bowls on the nearby green and might hear the slapping noises, so we decided instead to have another spanking session in his bedroom, with me bent over the end of his bed. He placed several mirrors around the room so I could watch myself being spanked. Very sexy. Normally, of course, it all goes on behind the spankee's head.

When this spanking session was over, rather bizarrely we decided to have a game of table tennis, since we both played and he had a table set up in a spare room. Strangely, it felt quite normal to be taking part in such an everyday activity after the abnormal (to me) goings-on of the past few hours. But I was gradually getting used to the various set-ups of my spankers. Each would have a slightly different agenda, a different mindset, a different goal when arranging a spanking session.

With the table tennis over, Jeremy didn't think I could take any more spanking, so asked me if I would like to join him for a meal in a nearby restaurant. He remarked that the day was turning out to be rather like a date. I agreed but started to realise what he was thinking. We did get on very well, and we had an important, fairly all-consuming hobby in common.

During the meal, he said it was lovely to have someone his age to talk to about spanking, as none of his family knew. Sometimes he longed to chat freely about one of his favourite pastimes, which was little understood by most people. I drove home rather elated after my day's exploits.

The next day I received an email from Jeremy saying how much he'd enjoyed our session and wondered if I'd like to go out on a real date. I liked him, and we had much in common, but he was just too far away. I'd tried long-distance relationships before and they were hard work. I had to decline this flattering offer and hoped that we could still be friends and spank. I was relieved that he continued to email me after that, and invite me up to his house for regular spankings.

That was sometimes the trouble with having single guys my age as spanking clients. If they asked me out on a date and I declined, which I invariably did, I often lost them as clients.

It was the first of many offers of dates from my spankers. It showed just how much the spankers view spankees as equals, as partners-in-crime, or should that be partners-in-fun. I was never patronised by my spankers outside of a spanking session. During spanking sessions, yes, they could be stern, rude, patronising, sarcastic, belittling – but that's all part of the role-play.

Chapter 8

My First Caning

I still wasn't sure if I wanted spankers to come to my house – a potentially great topic of gossip for the neighbours, but rather detrimental to my street cred. Or perhaps it would enhance it. I thought if I met the spankers first, I might let some of them come along to the house, as long as they disguised their implements. Standing on the doorstep with a cane poking out of their coat would cause an unacceptable level of intrigue. Home visits would obviously cut down my travelling costs and time taken for a session.

By the time I had been a spankee for a year, I had allowed three of them to visit my home. One came specifically to introduce me to the cane. He asked me to wear white stockings and suspenders for the session. He always turned up with a bunch of flowers, which touched me, especially at the beginning when I thought I was entering a near-prostitution scene. It seemed to show that despite my baring my bottom to strangers, he respected me.

He was a quietly spoken, middle-class, nice-looking man in his fifties. After the initial polite chit-chat and cup of tea, while I placed his flowers in water, he declared that not only was he going to cane me, but he also wanted to shave me if I would allow him to. I thought about it. It could do no harm. I might quite like it. I had met him a couple of times before, so I decided to go ahead. I could easily have declined. I never felt at any time in my 18 months as a spankee that I couldn't refuse to take part in any offered punishment.

He placed a towel on the armchair and asked me to lie on my

back on it with one leg on each arm of the chair. He had already removed my knickers, so everything was on display. He knelt down in front of me, took out a razor, dunked it in shaving cream and proceeded to shave my pubic region all over. Gradually I started to find it relaxing and erotic, once I'd got over the embarrassment of the revealing position in front of a strange man again.

I discovered that most spankers seem to want their spankees to be hairless down below. 'No hair below the eyelashes', one spanker said to me. The reason, he said, was because it makes the spankee look more feminine, more vulnerable, more innocent, more in need of discipline.

Then he asked to spank me over his knee on the sofa. After a lengthy, fairly firm hand-spanking to warm me up, which lasted a good five minutes, he requested the wheelbarrow position. This time I knew what it was, and I didn't feel as embarrassed as with the young guy. This man had just shaved me, after all, and he was only a few years younger than me. He had a wife and two grown-up children, was an experienced spanker, and must have seen all manner of shapes of vaginas. I began to relax. I also decided I liked being shaved. Not just the activity, which was quite erotic and relaxing, but the actual look. It was a bit like your armpits – nicer to behold when hairless. The spanking with his hand continued in the wheelbarrow position for about ten minutes. My bottom was very red and beginning to smart. Occasionally during the ten minutes, I told him it was too sore, and he stopped straight away and rubbed it, which brought immediate relief. After a minute or two of rubbing, the spanking continued.

Then he got up, took hold of the cane and in a half-humorous gesture, started swishing it through the air. He put it down and, taking my hand, led me through to the kitchen, where he had laid a cushion on the edge of the kitchen table. He told me to bend over the table over the cushion with legs together, my hands grasping the sides of the table and to wait for him there. I had to go on tiptoe to bend over it. It pushed my bottom up higher to present it for the caning.

I could hear him behind me fetching the cane from the other room, and then I was aware of him walking slowly back through into the kitchen, cane in hand. He took up a position to the left of me. He told me afterwards that my bare bottom was framed beautifully by the white stockings and suspenders. He said he would use the cane gently to begin with.

'Ready?' he asked quietly. I said I thought I was, very unconvincingly – but I knew I wanted to get used to the cane, as it's something most spankers seem to love. I thought I might be able to ask for more money if I could take it well.

I felt the cane being placed gently on my buttocks in readiness for the first stroke. My palms had begun to sweat and I remember looking at my kitchen table, two inches from my face and out of focus. I felt the cane being removed, and after a second heard the swish of it flying through the air and then a very sharp sting as it came down on both buttocks at once. *Ouch.* That was painful. But I wanted to try and take some more.

'Well done,' he said. 'Shall I go again? It's entirely up to you.'

'OK.'

I felt the cane placed on my bottom again. Seconds later came not one but two sharp strokes, one after the other, much harder than the first. I gasped at the pain. *Oh my god, the cane hurts!* Both strokes were so painful that I cried out, got up off the table, mumbled out loud, 'I can't take this' and marched through to the sitting room, where I sat in a fairly huffy, annoyed state. (That was probably breaking some tacit spankee rule, but I was past caring.)

He came through after me, rather concerned, and sat down beside me to calm me down. 'I know – it does hurt. Well done – you've just taken three strokes of the cane.'

I was embarrassed by my petulance and sudden, rather childish display of temper. I could have just said 'Ow' and said I didn't want any more, in a calm way. He was very understanding, but the atmosphere had changed slightly. I would have to watch my anger at pain inflicted in any future sessions, or I would lose clients. All the spankers I met just wanted a fun, consensual session between spanker and spankee. If I continued to flare up like that when the pain got too much, it would become unfun and awkward, and they would probably not return to me.

He remained polite, congratulated me again on taking the cane, reiterated that I had done well, and left. I wondered if I would see him again. (To my great relief, he hadn't been put off and became a regular.) I inspected the damage in the bathroom mirror. Several deep purple bruises were beginning to appear. It hurt to sit down. Did I really want to get used to such pain? I wasn't sure I did. How could other girls take it? Perhaps I could be a no-caning spankee.

I was disappointed by my behaviour, by the intense pain of the strokes, and by my intolerance. At the same time, my stubbornness and need to strive to do my best came to the fore. I knew I wanted to be able to tell people I could take whatever they wanted to throw at me – belts, straps, riding crops and, most importantly, the cane, the pinnacle of their excitement.

To my great relief, he came back several times after this first visit, and always used the cane. Over the course of his visits, I had become more accustomed to dealing with the cane from other spankers as well. I didn't enjoy the pain itself, but I liked the concept of being bent over to take the cane. I felt I was a proper spankee. He liked my bottom so much that during the first few visits, he took the photos below so that I would have proof of caning and to show me his handiwork.

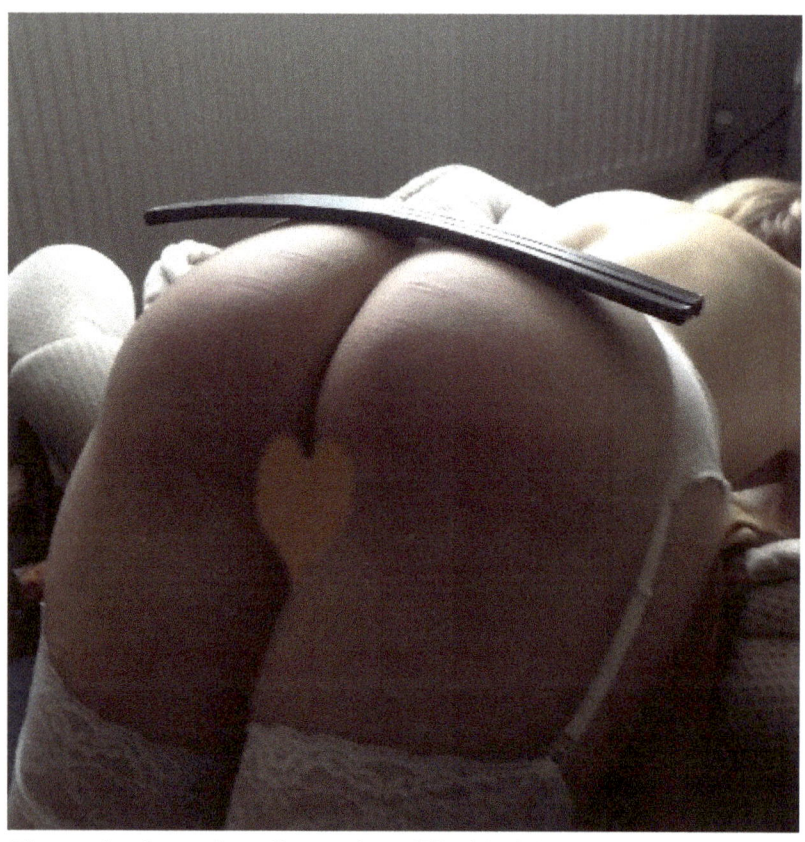

The result of one of my first canings. The black leather strap in the photo was used gently before the caning to warm up my bottom to prepare it for the cane. Photo by David Hepworth.'

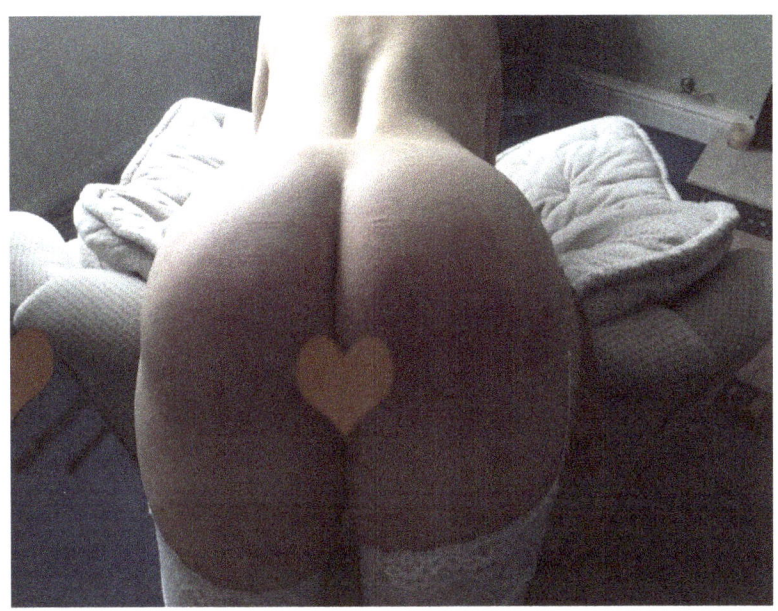

A rather distorted view of my caned bottom from a close camera shot. Photo by David Hepworth.

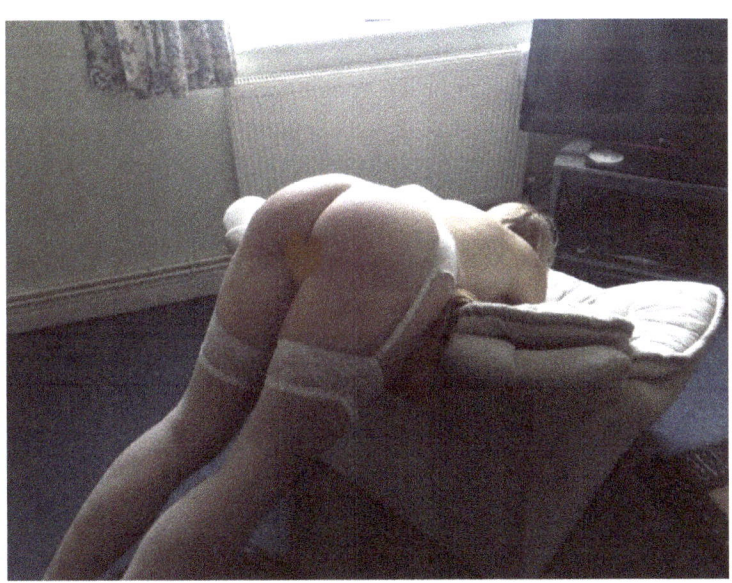

My soft armchair was a convenient height for spankings and canings. I sometimes joked that I could watch TV from there while the CP punishment carried on behind me. Photo by David Hepworth.

Chapter 9

Out of the Blue

One day, about three weeks into my spankeeship, I had an email from a well-educated, white male in his mid-forties who said he was looking for 'someone to spank regularly'. I will call him Blue. He was not interested in switching, as he was quite dominant, and mostly enjoyed bare-bottom over-the-knee spanking. He sent a photo, which surprised me. I could have done anything with it – put it on Facebook, for one thing. Not that I would dream of giving anyone's identity away, but Blue didn't know that. As it turned out, and as I got to know him over the following six months, he wouldn't have minded. Most people knew of his antics anyway, and he was proud of them. But there seems to be a tacit agreement among the CP community that you do not kiss and tell.

During our first few emails, Blue said he had never been married, did not have any children and didn't intend for either of those life events to happen in the future. I wondered what made someone decide on a life that solitary. It also made me wonder if he was a weird, axe-wielding recluse who just like to spank vulnerable women in his home and then bury them in the walls.

We arranged a date and time. I asked him what I should wear to meet him and if jeans were OK. He answered that he wanted me to wear whatever made me feel at ease. He then said he wanted me to get to know him as much as possible so I would feel relaxed in his company. I thought that was nice, but at this stage, I was still naïve or cautious enough to think that all spankers could be rapists and murderers, so was this approach a trick to lure me in?

My satnav had broken, so I decided to look at a map beforehand and memorise the route. I was to arrive at his house at 7.00 pm, without ever having met him or even spoken to him before. Was this crazy? I had so far not been wrong about my instincts about the spankers, going by their emails. A well-constructed, grammatically correct email meant to me that the emailer was likely to have a similar background to me and that we would be more likely to reach an understanding and have more fun together.

Having said that, I had sessions with brickies and A & E surgeons and had just as much fun with both. It was sometimes the tone of the email that made me wary, such as the abruptness with which they requested details of my rates and CP preferences. The chatty ones that said they didn't want to hurt me but just wanted to have some fun with me were more likely to receive a positive response from me.

At 7.05 pm, I was still driving along some dual carriageway a few miles from his house, trying to find somewhere to stop to explain that I hadn't, in fact, arrived, in case he hadn't noticed. Also that I didn't really know where I was, and so couldn't give him an ETA. I turned into a petrol station forecourt and, with some trepidation, phoned him. A very well-spoken, young-sounding male voice with a BBC accent answered.

'Hello. Where are you?' he asked, without establishing that it was me. I described where I had turned left down a Wellington Road.

'Right,' he said patiently, without any hint of irritation, 'turn round and just carry straight on until the High Street.'

He gave me a few more directions and I felt sure I had it straight in my mind. I set off, and about 40 minutes later, I was no nearer. A text came through: 'How are you doing?' I rang him, feeling like an idiot. I described my location, and he gave me further directions, saying at the end, 'Do you think you are going to be alright now?'

'Who knows?' I said.

He laughed and said I should be with him in a few minutes, all being well. I wondered if he thought I was just some dumb blonde.

At about 8.20 pm, still lost, I spotted a pub and rang him. 'Could you come and meet me? I've come into the car park of the White Swan.'

'Sure,' he said, 'be there in five minutes.'

Sure enough, within about five minutes, I saw a little white car with a missing hub-cap drive into the pub car park. A tall, slim guy looking no more than thirty got out and, looking quickly around, strode confidently towards me. Should I get out and kiss him? No, too forward. So I wound down my window and stuck my hand out, which he took with a smile. He seemed nice and friendly, even though I was by now one and half hours late.

I started blurting out that I thought it was easier for him to come and meet me. He waited patiently for me to finish my sentence and then just said, 'Sure. You follow me.' I followed his car in the dark to a small residential back street in the centre of the city. Cars lined both sides of the road, with few gaps, so we had to park in spaces about 100 yards apart.

I got out, and up the road I could see Blue's tall, slim, silhouetted frame against the street lamps waiting for me. This is it, I thought. I could run for it, but knew I wasn't going to. I walked towards him and then followed him into his house. The house seemed to have bare floorboards and little furniture. I felt slightly uneasy, but he'd been very kind on the phone, and was now offering me a cup of tea, which I accepted. I said I needed to go to the loo, and he said, 'I thought you might. I made one earlier for you.' I chuckled at this reference to the famous quote from the Blue Peter demonstrations from my childhood, and started to feel further at ease.

When I came downstairs, he handed me a cup of tea and sat on the sofa next to me but a little way away. He asked me why I had started being a spankee, and I saw for the first time how handsome he was. His photo didn't do him justice. We chatted about the spanking scene, and then he suddenly said, 'I like you. I'd like to see you often. We can develop a good interaction and do more than just spank. I will spank you regularly and pay you every now and then.

We can have so much more fun than just a spanker-spankee relationship. What do you think?'

I was flattered by this offer but didn't know quite what he meant. Did he mean a relationship? He was twelve years younger than me, and I hadn't contemplated dating any of the spankers, since I'd been told by a fellow spankee that the vast majority of spankers are married and just want some harmless fun, which suited me fine. But I didn't want to offend him so early on in the evening, so I just said, 'I like you too. Er – that sounds interesting.'

Then his attitude changed slightly. He got up, sat down next to me and put his hand on my thigh. 'I will need you to be naked now,' he said in a way that wasn't really a request. The room was brightly lit. No gentle, soft light to make my body look anything other than 57, despite the fact that I did have an excellent body for my age. Did he want me to undress like a stripper while he watched?

It was all rather surreal. He could have been asking me if I wanted another cup of tea. Instead, he wanted me naked in front of him, as if it was the most natural thing in the world. I suddenly felt embarrassed and inexperienced, and said, 'I think you will have to help me.'

'OK – stand up,' he commanded. He stood behind me and bent over me. He reached round from behind, unzipped my jeans and pulled them down to my knees without hesitation. Then he bent over me from behind again, and said, 'By the way – I'm OK. You don't know me, but I am OK.'

It was a relief to hear this, although I had already decided that he probably was safe to be with.

He pulled down my knickers to where the jeans were around my knees, and then took off my jumper, T-shirt and bra. He sat down on the sofa again, and roughly pulled me over his knee, where he proceeded to give my bottom about ten quite firm slaps with his hand. A few on one buttock, and then the other. He then pulled off my boots, jeans, socks and knickers, and I lay there across this stranger's knee, naked and utterly vulnerable, with only my instincts that I had developed over years of meeting people to guide me.

But I have to say that it began to feel surprisingly right – and very exciting. He was quite a hard spanker and I started to complain about the pain. He immediately stopped each time for a while, and rubbed my buttocks, bringing instant relief. When we got to know each other later, he told me he'd never known a sub complain so much. He had a way of giving an extra-long massage stroke just before the spanking started again, so I grew to recognise the signs of the impending resumption of smacks even during that first encounter.

We changed positions a few times, from the sofa to over his knee on a chair in the middle of the room, where my feet and hands hung down in mid-air on either side of him. Throughout the spankings, he would chat to me amicably, as if we were discussing the weather. But when anything to do with spanking came up, there would emerge a dominant character that I found hard to argue with, although feeling confident that I could at any time get dressed and walk out of the house. It was a world of make-believe, where he became a dominant, and I got to play a submissive. And I was being paid. This was really quite easy money.

'Want to try the riding crop and cane?' he asked at one point. I agreed rather hesitantly, more out of curiosity regarding the riding crop, so he told me to kneel on the sofa, with my hands on the back of the sofa, and to stick my bottom out. I felt suddenly vulnerable, bent over naked in front of man with a cane – but wasn't that part of the attraction? I also felt confident that I was 'safe' with him, and that if I said 'stop', he would. I never discussed a 'safe' word with him (or any of the spankers I met, for that matter) if the pain became too much. Unlike in films, he just said that I was to tell him if I wanted him to stop, and he would do so immediately. I believed him.

He took a lethal-looking black riding crop out of a holder in the room and started sliding it down my back and over my already red bottom. Then I felt a light but sharp whipping pain on both buttocks. He gave me two strokes of the crop, but having been spanked quite hard for about an hour by then, my tolerance level was subsiding, and I said I didn't want any more.

'OK. We'll try the cane.'

He went back to the holder, while I waited naked on the sofa. Out came a beige-coloured cane, seemingly made with a light, smooth bamboo or wicker, with a large curved handle, just like you would imagine a headmaster would use. He laid it gently across my bottom and said, 'Ready?'

It was just one light stroke, but the pain was intense. I had had enough and decided I didn't want to be spanked or caned or have any further implements used on my very red bottom that evening. I turned round and looked at him, and hoped to god he was going to oblige.

'I think I've had enough now, you know.'

'OK. Well done. You did very well.'

The cane and riding crop were returned to the holder. To do otherwise would have been tantamount to abuse in the eyes of the law.

I assumed the evening was over, but he suddenly grabbed me and hauled me bodily over his knee again over the sofa, saying what a sexy girl I was. He asked if he could put his hand between my legs. I was taken aback by his boldness, since none of the other spankers had suggested sex, but it didn't alarm me. I was incredibly turned on by the whole experience.

'Yes, OK,' I said. He pushed my legs wide apart. His fingers were experienced and I just lay there, revelling in this astonishingly sexy, exciting turn of events. He asked if I would go upstairs with him and have sex.

'Do you normally have sex with your spankees?' I asked him, looking back at him over my shoulder from my prostrate position.

'Only with two of them,' he stated matter-of-factly, looking at me intently. It made me aware again how closely sex and spanking can be interlinked. Inside I was thinking, 'Oh my God, this guy is paying me, and asking me for sex. How close am I from entering the dark world of prostitution?' But I didn't feel threatened by him.

I was also flattered. He was a good-looking, strong, fit guy, 12 years my junior. He'd seen my 57-year-old body in a brightly lit room – and still wanted sex. I didn't want to end the evening on a refusal and, in fact, didn't know at the time whether I wouldn't have sex with him at a later session, if I got to know him and we started a relationship. So I just said, 'Well, maybe – another time.' He accepted this reply with good grace.

Then he told me to get dressed and said he would take me back to the motorway (three miles away) 'to ensure you reach home by morning.' He handed me an envelope with £90 in it. Although we had agreed a price of £70, he said he had added £20 for the petrol I had wasted trying to find him. I thought of counting it and then decided quickly that that would be inappropriate. I hesitated slightly though. I thought we had agreed to £70 for the first hour, and then £50 per hour after that pro-rata. Blue had thought it was £70 for the whole session, however long that turned out to be.

He noticed my hesitation. 'We agreed £70. You should make sure you are clear about your charges before you meet clients,' he said sternly.

'Oh – no, that's fine,' I said quickly, bowing to his experience and not wishing to ruin the evening.

Before I left, he suddenly stepped towards me and put his arms round me. I was fully dressed by then, and I was surprised by this sudden show of affection. It was as if we were about to have a slow dance. 'My real name is _____,' he said, smiling. For some reason, it hadn't occurred to me that spankers would also use false names. I had used a fake name on the website, as I didn't want to be recognised. I told him my real name in return. The dominant, commanding spanker had disappeared, and was replaced by the nice, polite guy who had met me in the pub car park. Just a lovely, ordinary, considerate, funny guy who made me laugh so easily.

I asked him at one point towards the end of the evening if he wasn't worried that a completely strange woman now knew his address and could stalk him.

'No,' came the immediate reply, 'because that particular woman would have to ring up for directions.'

*****

So began a spanker-spankee interaction that lasted six months, that let me into an intimate dom-sub world and allowed me to meet one of the nicest, most patient, most intelligent and humorous men I'd ever met.

I didn't hear from Blue for two weeks and supposed that I hadn't come up to his expectations as a spankee, with my complaints and refusal to have sex with him. But then he texted to say he'd like to see me again. I knew I liked him more than just as a client spanker, but because of the age difference I didn't want to admit it even to myself. We arranged for him to come to my house. I live in a cul-de-sac in a quiet country village where neighbours can easily see other people's visitors, and the last thing I wanted was a string of men queueing outside my house, cane in hand. Blue said he would disguise the implements under his coat, and anyway, wasn't he the only spanking visitor? Yes, at the moment he was. I hadn't decided how many men I would allow to visit concurrently.

He turned up at my house with no implements I was relieved to see. When I greeted him in the hallway, I found myself suddenly wanting to kiss him.

'I nearly kissed you,' I confided to him.

'Well, why don't you?' he said immediately, and bent down to give me a slow kiss on the mouth. And without wasting any more time on small talk, he continued, 'Now you can come over to the sofa and we'll see if you can take any more than last time.'

'I was going to make you a cup of tea,' I started to say, but in a trice, he had me over his knee, jeans and knickers down to my knees, and was spanking my bottom with such a sting that I cried out. He caressed my buttocks for a few seconds and then continued the hand spanking. He had no doubt been imagining doing that as he drove to my house.

Looking back now, I can see that he was only ever interested in the spanking and sexual side of our relationship. I, on the other hand, still on the lookout for a soulmate to replace Pen, saw him as a potential partner.

After about five minutes, he said, 'Let's try you over the back of the armchair.' He turned the armchair round, led me into position at the back of the chair, and continued to undress me until I was completely naked again in front of him, while he remained dressed beside me, looking down at me. I found out later that this scenario (called MDFN – male dressed, female naked) is all part of the dom-sub scene. The sub is vulnerable, naked, slightly humiliated and at the mercy of the dom, who is supposedly in control, dressed, not humiliated and deciding the fate of his sub.

'Bend over,' Blue ordered quietly. I bent over the back of the armchair, and felt his hand press down on my head so that my feet came off the floor. I had to use my hands to steady myself on the two arms of the chair. I did feel vulnerable, as intended, and sexy come to that. 'You are such a sexy girl,' he murmured.

He started to spank me hard, one slap on one reddening cheek then the next slap on the other. I complained and he stopped each time, caressed me and then continued.

'Spread your legs,' he commanded. I did so. 'Wider.'

I spread them wider, and felt his fingers caress my lips again. 'I've brought a durex in case you change your mind, you know.'

I thought about it. Would it do any harm? It was so deliciously rude being bent over the armchair, being felt up and spanked hard like this. Also, we hadn't mentioned payment, so I could justify this as an ordinary, non-prostitute-like sexual act between myself and a potential partner. And why would I need to justify anything? If I wanted to have sex, who's going to know or care?

'Go on then.'

'Yeah?' and quickly, he got a condom out of his pocket and

slipped it on. He started penetrating me, but I hadn't had sex in a while so it was hurting. I had to ask him to stop a few times, which he immediately did, but in the end, he came all the way into me.

'Do you always carry condoms with you?' I asked afterwards.

'Mostly yes. And I always practise safe sex, even if I know the girl well. And I don't come in the vagina normally. I only come in the rectum. We'll have to try that with you soon.'

I wasn't so sure about that. I had tried it twice as a teenager and got nowhere fast because of the discomfort. To my mind, anuses are not designed to have objects shoved up them. The other direction is the only one nature intended. He was so matter-of-fact about this, as if discussing the type of weather we were having. I was to notice this often with other spankers. They talked about spanking, sex, genitals, orgasms, even excrement, with utter seriousness, and no hint of embarrassment or self-conscious giggles or smiles. Mention the word 'spanking' to the normal man/woman in the street and a smile will almost invariably start to appear on their face.

Blue came to my house frequently after that. On arrival, he would take my face in his hands and kiss me fervently. I noticed him swallowing a few times when he first arrived and took that to mean that he really liked me. I was growing increasingly fond of him, but didn't like to admit it even to myself. He was twelve years younger, for goodness sake.

The initial kissing over, we would chat for a while and then I would often be hauled over his knee on the sofa, skirt lifted up and knickers taken down, and given a firm spanking. He had suggested we do this mostly for fun, but that every now and then he would pay me for my services so that he could ask me to act like a proper spankee, at his command. I declined to be paid by a man who was becoming a friend and boyfriend, which I think pleased him. Not because of the money, but because it meant I was liking being with him, and being spanked by him on a regular basis.

It emerged that he had envisaged having a dom-sub relationship with me after seeing me on the internet. He wanted to train me to be his sub. I noticed that his attitude when spanking me was changing subtly to be more commanding. He started telling me to stand in the corner or face one of the walls after a spanking so that he could see my red bottom on display.

I still had a bad back from crash landing under a parachute about 20 years previously. Standing still for more than about five minutes made my back ache. On one occasion, while I was standing in the corner of my sitting room, completely naked, facing the wall, unable to see what he was doing, or whether he was still in fact in the room, he would sometimes make himself a cup of tea and deliberately not make me one – all part of the game of domination and humiliation of a submissive. He would come in from the kitchen with his cup of tea and accuse me of having moved from the position he had placed me in. He would make me use the word 'Sir' when speaking to him. I understood the idea behind this, but the more I got to know him as a friend and lover, the more I started to feel silly using it.

'Did I put you in that position?' he would bark.

'No, Sir.'

'Come here.'

And I would be told to place myself across his knee and be spanked again, often with thirty or more hard slaps. So sexy, even though at times quite painful.

The dom-sub interaction progressed slowly with each visit to my house. He would find issues with my recent behaviour, such as cancelling a visit, even though there was an unavoidable reason for it, and proclaim that I needed to be punished with a sound spanking. One particular time I texted him to say I would have to cancel due to work. He texted back, *'OK, that's fine.'* Then five minutes later, *'Don't think I'm going to forget this.'* A shiver of excitement went through me when I read this. Just before he arrived at my house on the following visit, he texted, *'When you open the door to me, I want you to be naked.'*

When he arrived at my house, he wasn't smiling. I duly answered the door, completely naked, and slightly hiding behind the door so the neighbours couldn't see. He came in, closed the door, marched through to the kitchen, grabbed one of the hard chairs and took it back into the sitting room. He came over to me where I was standing naked watching him, and walked me to the chair, where he sat down and pulled me over his knee.

'Now,' he said sternly, 'I was disappointed with your behaviour this week, do you hear?'

'Yes,' I said, slightly flustered and nervous.

'Yes what?'

'Yes, Sir.'

'I don't like being let down like that.'

Silence from me. Then I decided to say something. 'I couldn't help it. It was work.'

'You can cancel on me whenever you like but I won't like it and you can expect to be punished.' And with that, he proceeded to slap my bottom hard for one or two minutes continuously so that it started to sting.

It was slightly unnerving having this changing character in my house. Even though I knew it was all play-acting for the thrill of the spanking scenario, and I knew I could put an end to it at any moment, I did sometimes wonder if I was doing the right thing.

He slipped seamlessly into his role as a dom, having been in amateur dramatics and being quite a theatrical character anyway. I was not a natural actress. I felt self-conscious playing this role with someone who I had started to view as a boyfriend, and who I knew in twenty minutes would turn into a nice, kind, non-dominating guy, who I could snuggle with on the sofa and watch a film.

He would stop for minutes at a time, while instructing me how to behave like a proper sub. Then the spanking would continue. And all of a sudden, he would decide that the punishment was over. He'd ask me to get up from being bent over his knee and to stand next to him, where I expected to be spanked again. Then he would gently sit me down on his knee and there he was, back again, the guy I was dating. He would start to smile and laugh, and say I had done well, and taken a good spanking.

I was always conscious of the neighbours being able to hear the spanking noises. I had been told by someone who organises spanking parties that if he ventured outside into his garden while spanking was taking place, he could easily hear the slaps. After that, I worried about my immediate neighbours in our semi-detached houses hearing everything through the thin walls. I became slightly obsessed by this, which ruined some of the impromptu spanking positions I would find myself in as soon as Blue came through the door on his visits.

In our excitement at seeing each other and the thought of an imminent spanking over the armchair, we would greet each other at the door, come straight into the sitting room where Blue would take me immediately over his knee without much conversation, take down my trousers and knickers in a trice and start spanking me, only for me to remember that we hadn't closed the doors that led to either the kitchen or the hall, which meant that the neighbours were only one wall away from the slapping noise. I would suddenly say in mid-spank 'The door!' and Blue would have to stop and let me get up off his knee, waddle with trousers round my ankles to the doors, shut them, and waddle back to put myself back over his knee, to allow him to carry on spanking. All of this took control away from him as the dom, and often killed the mood. Once or twice he just stopped and said the moment had passed. This left me feeling hugely disappointed, as well as guilty for having failed as a sub once more to allow him the tantalising immediacy of an unplanned and sexy spanking as soon as he walked through the door.

He said once that with other girls with whom he'd had relationships, and whom he had been able to spank as part of the relationship, he had sometimes been able to walk through the door, take their knickers down, spank them and have sex with them on the stairs. I was too clinical, he stated, and too preoccupied with the neighbours, or objects on the sofa, or on the armchair, for him to feel he could indulge in impromptu, raw spanking and sex. I was hurt by this but recognised that he was probably right. And for all my worries that the neighbours would hear, they probably heard anyway. And they probably didn't care. It's not against the law, as long as there are only consenting adults taking part.

In general though, I was becoming a good sub, and he made me feel proud of my progression. One half of me actually *was* proud, while the other half couldn't believe what I was doing. This was absurd, wasn't it? To stand in the corner and be treated like a naughty schoolgirl? Absurd, yes, but somehow deliciously sexy and rude.

During my six months with Blue, I was starting to see other spankers who had contacted me through the web page. It was becoming less frightening and less strange with each contact to meet complete strangers, to go to a lodge or hotel (which they always paid for without question) and be spanked, belted, thrashed quite hard with paddles, riding crops or straps, as well as the occasional caning, while they chatted to me quite amicably and sometimes fingered my labia.

Blue would be very interested in these encounters. He wanted to know every detail I was willing to tell him. I think a small part of him was jealous, but he never told me that in words. I could see it in his expression. He wanted to know if they had played with my crotch, and what positions they had placed me in, how hard they had smacked me, and with what implements. After all, he had no way of knowing how other spankers behaved unless he asked spankees, since he didn't go to spanking parties.

He suggested on more than one occasion that once I had paid off my £20,000 debt that I might stop seeing other spankers, which made me realise that he indeed did like me – or perhaps it was just the ownership issue rearing its ugly head. You can hardly be a dominant and simultaneously want your sub to be shared with other men.

On one occasion, I emerged from a session with a particularly zealous spanker with several purple and blue bruises on my backside from the cane. Blue happened to be visiting two days later. He took one look at the bruises, and instead of abstaining from touching me as I thought he would, he started spanking me as normal. I was surprised it didn't hurt more than usual, but I guess a spanking stings the surface, whereas the cane bruises more deeply below the surface.

After a few minutes of continuous spanking, I realised that it was going on longer than normal, and he wasn't being his usual chatty self. I began to complain about the severity.

'Taking the cane from someone else is a punishable crime,' he said. 'You are my sub, and I am going to leave my mark on you.'

'No, Blue, you're hurting me now!'

He stopped, and started to rub my bottom for me. He let me up, and we started making a cup of tea. But he was still ominously quiet. Then he tried to grab me again, to put me over his knee again, but I had had enough. I managed to escape his grip and dashed upstairs, locking myself in the bathroom. He followed me upstairs and banged on the door.

'Open the door!' he ordered.

'No!'

'Open the door now!' he commanded again.

'No! I can't take any more tonight.'

This wasn't what I had signed up for. It was slightly scary, even though I knew he was still officially in dom mode. After a few seconds, he said, 'I'm going now, but I won't forget this.'

I heard his footsteps going downstairs, and then heard the front door being opened and closed gently. I stayed in the bathroom for about ten minutes, thinking that he could have pretended to leave but still be in wait for me downstairs.

'This is utterly ridiculous,' I thought. 'This is taking it too far.' But half of me was quite excited at the prospect of the next encounter with him, and I was also flattered that he minded that someone had got to cane me properly before him.

I gingerly opened the bathroom door and crept very slowly downstairs. I seriously didn't want to be spanked again for a few days. Blue had gone. I was thankfully left alone to lick my wounds.

I didn't agree to see him again until my bruises had gone. When he arrived, he didn't mention the bathroom caper, but had unusually brought a riding crop. He ordered me upstairs to the bedroom, told me to undress completely and lie face down on the bed. He berated me for leaving him outside on the doorstep too long (any excuse). I had been upstairs in the shower and hadn't heard his knock on the door. He then whipped me with the riding crop quite gently about ten times. This was easy to take, but I wondered what was coming. He commanded me to lie on my back naked and lift my legs in the air wide apart. He stood over me and whipped my buttocks again, then caressed my lips with the crop, then suddenly whipped my upturned feet so that I cried out. Then he whipped my buttocks again.

'Ow!' I cried out again, slightly annoyed. The spell was broken, and he instantly turned into non-spanker guy. 'Do you want a cup of tea?' he asked, a little too quietly.

'Why did you stop?' I asked, disappointed, but in fact I knew the reason why. I had shown irritation at the pain, which was not part of a sub's role.

'Because you are not entering into the spirit of it. You are not embracing the notion of being a submissive. Submissives don't get annoyed. They take what their doms give them.'

'But it hurt,' I said, rather deflated by my lack of success as a sub, but also wondering if I was suited to any kind of dom-sub activity.

'There are ways to let me know, you know, without getting annoyed. I will never harm you intentionally. The punishment will sting, because that's the whole point of a spanking. But I wouldn't harm you for the world. You have to trust me. I am your dom. You are in my care. You have to entrust your welfare to me completely. I am training you as a sub. I chose you from the beginning because I believe we can have a wonderful interaction as dom and sub. Don't throw this opportunity away. For example, stop watching what I am doing with the riding crop as if you don't trust me.'

'Well, I don't,' I said truthfully.

'Then you are not embracing this interaction and it might not work between us.' Ridiculous to say, I felt ashamed that I had let him down. 'I cannot do this if you don't fully understand what we are doing,' he went on. 'If you undermine me by coming out of sub mode, like you did just now by getting annoyed, the whole scene with me as dominant is eroded and we are left as two silly adults playing around. You have to submit to me fully, and you will see the benefits. We can have such fun and such exciting sex if you embrace this properly.'

We carried on drinking our tea, making awkward conversation. Then he got up and I could see he was in dom mode once more. I was inordinately pleased that he was giving me another chance. This time I was determined to play the part. I allowed the riding crop whippings, which grew harder with each stroke, and answered 'Yes Sir' and 'No Sir' in appropriate places, while he continued the tirade against my behaviour as a wayward sub.

That night I thought about what he had said. I would have to decide either to enter the dom-sub world wholeheartedly, or leave it. He was keeping to his side of the bargain. It was he who had to conjure up 'issues' between us that would make a punishment imperative. It was he who had to think up different positions to place me in and articulate the reasons for his 'disappointment', emphasising the expected behaviour of a sub. If I was going to be too self-conscious or tetchy to join in properly, and continue to be 'me', he was right – it was pointless and a waste of time, and made him look like an idiot.

He kidded me that I was the worst sub in the world, and although I knew he was trying to say it in a jokey way, it was starting to gall between us. I didn't want to lose him. I had started to feel I could love him. So I decided to go all out and try and be a good sub. I texted him this decision.

'What's brought this on?' he texted back.
'I thought I would just try and be a good sub for once.'
'Good girl.'

I wasn't sure if I really liked the patronising-sounding 'good girl' or the term 'young lady' that he often called me (slightly bizarre since I was 12 years his senior), but for the time being, I would take all that being a sub entailed, launching myself into the next few months of raw spanking and sex. I tried to forget about the relationship side, hoping that that would emerge as a side-effect of this new, spectacular, raunchy dom-sub interaction.

Blue brought up the subject of anal sex again, which he had alluded to on his first visit. We had tried it once before over the armchair rather unsuccessfully, and I had hoped he wouldn't want to try again. Anal penetration hurt, and did nothing for me sexually, as I know it can do for some women. But he had stated several times that he could never orgasm in a vagina, only ever in the rectum. He said he found sex in the vagina 'too normal, not special enough'.

'Don't take this the wrong way,' he said to me once, 'but loads of men have been up your vagina. It's about ownership. I want something of you that no one else has ever had.'

I understood this notion, and despite not liking the concept of ownership, I accepted it within the context of our dom-sub relationship. But I sometimes doubted that it was for him strictly within the CP boundary that he needed to own part of me. I liked that he wanted something unique with me however, so in theory I knew I was going to give anal sex a go, but kept hoping it was never 'tonight'.

Blue and I did other things apart from spank, even during this supposed intense dom-sub period. We played singles badminton and discovered that we had a similar standard. Some of our rallies went on for minutes and we ended up utterly breathless with laughter. We also went out to restaurants, and to the cinema. We would watch films on TV and snuggle on the sofa (although he would often fall asleep and leave me watching on my own, which defeated the object from my point of view.) It was to all intents and purposes a relationship, as far as I was concerned.

We had another thing in common – bereavement, and its effect on your life. Blue had lost both his parents in his mid-thirties, as well as four friends to various diseases within the space of six years. Like me, it had left him with a dread of wasting time before his final breath. He took it one stage further. He refused to take part in group activities, even groups of three including himself, saying that it was too stressful to make conversation with more than one person. People try to outdo each other with knowledge and witty repartee, was his argument. For this reason, he only ever saw his friends one by one. He hated being forced to go to places in which he had no interest, as this was also using up valuable time. I, too, had begun to avoid group situations much more after Pen's death, and it was a relief to discover that someone else felt the same.

One hot evening in summer, after we had been playing singles badminton, and just as we were getting into our respective cars, I noticed some thick bushes and small patches of woodland surrounding the car park. I suddenly felt sweaty and lusty, and suggested we have sex among them, to which Blue readily agreed. There were not that many trees, and you could see daylight through them to the road beyond but we hoped in our sudden randiness that we wouldn't be detected.

We found a little clearing inside a particularly thick slice of woodland, with a birch tree in just the right position for me to lean up against. Blue wasted no time, as usual. He had my shorts and knickers down to my ankles and pushed me over, so that I could lean against the tree. But after a lot of pushing and shoving, we decided it wasn't really going to work, mainly due to our relative heights. Then Blue suggested we try anal sex again. I wasn't too enamoured with the idea, but was willing to try it again.

Surprisingly he didn't try spanking me, the normal prelude to sex, designed to turn us both on. This was more a technical issue. He used lubrication and gently put two fingers inside my anus. It felt uncomfortable, as if I needed the bathroom. He did this for a few minutes and then tried with his condom-covered penis. It felt as if he were trying to shove a large cucumber up my bottom, and I remember thinking, 'There's no way it's going up there.' He was being very gentle and careful, but it was beginning to hurt. Slowly, slowly he was inching into my rectum, but I was very tight, probably through nerves, and it just wouldn't go in. We tried twice more, with not much more success.

'Let's try one last time,' he said, rather resigned, 'and then we'll give up.'

I reluctantly agreed. I knew that this was the ultimate in sexual stimulation for him. In went the lubricated fingers, and then the seemingly huge penis that felt like it would split me apart. Suddenly I felt my anus widen, and he edged in a bit more. Then it widened again, and he was fully in. Now, apart from feeling the pressure against the side of the rectum, I couldn't feel him inside at all. It was as if he were moving around in a void. How peculiar. And how comical to have lost my anal virginity in a sports hall car park, with traffic going to and fro yards from our tree. There was no pain, just a rather uncomfortable full feeling.

Then I noticed the strangest noises coming from behind. Blue was uttering low, breathless grunts and roaring noises like I'd never heard before. Within a minute or so, they reached such a crescendo that I thought people in the car park would hear. It was all over in about ten seconds and I felt him withdraw slowly. I was slightly concerned that this action would take the rectal lining with it, but it seemed to remain intact. After all, gays seem to survive it, so I suppose I would.

I looked around at him. He had a happy, breathless, spent look on his handsome face, with not a shred of embarrassment about the noise level. I felt very proud that I was the reason.

I had opened the floodgates. Blue wanted anal sex all the time after that. I did like him a lot, and wanted him to enjoy sex with me, so I wanted to like it too, and hoped that it would get easier with time. Well, it certainly got easier with time – but I didn't grow to like it. After a month or so, after the normal hand-spanking over the back of the armchair, he barely had to use his fingers to lubricate me, and my rectum started to allow him to enter almost straight away. The bull-like noises were sometimes so loud that I had to ask him to keep it down because of the neighbours.

But I had started to dread it. I realised that I wasn't looking forward to him coming to my house as much as I had been. I knew I would be spanked, quite hard, probably harder than I really liked, and that I would then be asked to bend over the armchair naked so that he could sodomise me. We often didn't have vaginal sex at all, although he would have if I had asked for it. I found it hard to enjoy vaginal sex, knowing I was about to be sodomised, so I chose to go straight to the anal sex to get it out the way as soon as possible. Then I would be able to snuggle on the sofa with him, and tell myself we were having a normal relationship.

It was about this time that a very small incident happened between us that I never forgot – it was the start of my doubts about whether I wanted to continue the relationship. I had bought a flowering basket and wanted to hang it up outside my house. There was a hook nailed to the roof of the porch outside my front door. I couldn't quite reach it, so when Blue arrived, I asked him if he would just hang it up on the hook for me. At 5' 11", it was no problem for him. The weight of the basket was minimal. I could lift it quite easily. But he looked at me with a definite expression of irritation.

'I don't like to be asked things like this. These are things you would ask a boyfriend. It's like asking me to go and visit your mother. I'm not here to waste my time doing chores around your house.'

He eventually hung it up for me and went into the house, disgruntled. How ridiculous, I thought. And how unkind. It literally took him two seconds to hang it up. I would have had to fetch a chair from inside the house and stand on it to hang the basket up. I was not impressed and filed it away at the back of my mind for future assessment.

I was beginning to realise just how uninterested he was in the 'let's be a cosy family unit' side of our relationship. He was also terribly afraid of being ill and dying, due to his parents' sudden demise, resulting in a deep desire not to waste a second of life unnecessarily. Doing other people's chores were wasted seconds. No one can say how losing both parents would affect them, but I think I would have been pleased to help someone for two seconds.

We discussed spanking outside, as we had both enjoyed the odd sexual encounter al fresco, so we waited for a very dark, warm night and then drove into a field near my home. I was wearing green wellies and a billowy, yellow dress. We got out and Blue pulled off my dress and pushed me over the car bonnet. Bra and knickers were removed in a trice, but I insisted on keeping my wellies on. He took off his belt and thrashed my bottom with it about twenty times quite hard as I lay over the bonnet, completely naked but for my green wellies, bottom raised and breasts resting against the warm car. While I clung to the top of the bonnet, he took me from behind, and lay on top of me for a while, panting and elated. It was a very sexy moment.

I had started noticing that the skin on my backside was becoming much thicker and rougher, which enabled me to take harder and harder spankings, beltings, and canings, and to enjoy them more. The Heathrow guy, who had become a regular, gave up after one spanking and said it was obviously hurting his hand far more than it was hurting me. Blue was able to spank me, then cane me, then give me a belting of a hundred strokes (he sometimes counted).

'You've become a phenomenal spankee,' he remarked once. I was so proud.

One day we were sitting watching TV together when I said I had to go to the bathroom. He asked if I was going to have a poo, and I said I was.

'Can I come and watch and wipe your bottom afterwards? Or perhaps I could manually evacuate your bowels?'

'What? Christ, no. No, you certainly can't!' I was disgusted.

'OK. No worries. It's not a huge fetish of mine. It's just about ownership. I would know that I had done something that no other man has done with you.' Then he added as a passing comment, 'I did it with my previous girlfriend.'

'Whooaaa! You did WHAT?' I had to hear about this one! Apparently, he had asked her the same thing and she had agreed, after a little persuasion. So he had sat on the edge of the bath while she had a poo in the loo. When she finished, without looking at her poo, she just put herself over his knee where he sat on the bath and let him wipe her bottom clean. That happened twice. On another occasion, she let him manually evacuate her bowels with two fingers. Fascinated that there are people in the world with such outrageous fetishes, I couldn't help asking if she had still needed to have a poo afterwards. 'No,' he answered proudly, with a mock American accent, 'I evacuated her real good.'

Yes, well, that's as may be, but being a poo extractee was not on my web page – or on my long-term radar.

After two or three months, I noticed changes in Blue's behaviour. When he came through the door on his visits, he stopped looking nervous, stopped swallowing when he tried to speak, and worst of all, to me, he stopped trying to kiss me hello. He started saying we were having an interaction, not a relationship. I hated the idea of what I had with Blue as not being a relationship. I mentioned the lack of kissing and he said he wasn't really a kissing type of person.

'Well, you were at the beginning,' I commented.

'People often do things out of character at the beginning of relationships, and then after a few weeks settle down to their normal selves,' he retorted.

I wasn't entirely convinced or happy with this explanation, but I had to accept it for the time being. He also said at about this time that he wasn't at all romantic, wasn't sure what love was; thought he had only been in love once and wasn't looking for it again. I took that admission to be an excuse as to why he felt he would never love me. He said snuggling on the sofa was 'OK', but he could take it or leave it.

One day I asked him by text if he would like to go to London for the day to see the London Eye. He texted back, *'OK.'* I commented that he didn't sound very enthusiastic. He said he loved his everyday life so much that he didn't want to disrupt it for a day by sitting on a train for hours, waiting in queues, only to have to do the same journey at the end of the day. He also said he wouldn't want to go on day trips to any city, and especially not three-day European city breaks, which I had hinted I loved. The hassle of waiting at airports, packing, preparing his work and life before the holiday and then catching up on return rendered it too stressful to be worth the effort, according to Blue.

At about this time, we had what we came to call the 'sofa conversation'. We had the normal spanking session, had had a meal and were just settling down to watch TV. He suddenly became quite serious and turned to me on the sofa and said that he knew I was looking for a long-term boyfriend and that he would never be it. He would never be the 'real deal'. He would never want to meet my friends or my family or want to go for afternoon trips to see a National Trust house. He was utterly happy to see me for what we did and didn't want anything else. This consisted of the following: spanking, sodomy, meals out and in, cinema and singles badminton. And that was it. Nothing else – apart from maybe a lesson in golf from him – was ever going to change or develop about my life with Blue. He wanted me to be completely warned about what he wanted from, and for, me.

'What we have is pure,' he said, straightforwardly. 'I will never have to resent you because I have to go and drink tea with your mother or spend time doing something I don't want to do because you want me to do it. I'm with you now because I really like you and want to be with you.'

It was clear he would never love me, although I think in his own way, he was very fond of me. He admitted that he 'very much liked my company' and would miss me if I wasn't around. He did make time for me in the week, I realised, but how much of that was because he had a very high libido and needed sex?

I was finding it easier and easier to let him into my anus, although I still didn't enjoy it. It didn't turn me on, and there was no sexual feeling to it for me, like for some girls. I did it to keep him around because I had feelings for him, although I could never really let myself fall completely in love with him because I knew it wouldn't be reciprocated. I sometimes felt like a convenience for him.

He explained once that he had many friends, and he did many different things with all of them. With one, he could play badminton, with another he could watch DVDs, with another he would watch the football. But he couldn't have sex with any of them, so that's what he liked about me. Gee, thanks. I said relationships were about more than sex. They were about companionship, sharing experiences, closeness. He said he had enough people in his life already who loved him and cared for him. He didn't need closeness with a woman. He had companionship, shared experiences and closeness with his friends. A most extraordinary outlook on life. I didn't know whether to envy him or pity him. But it wasn't my job to do either. He wasn't asking for my approval for this approach. He was just explaining it to me so that I would understand where I fitted into his life. What sort of weird, emotionally-challenged robot had I unearthed? He said he was glad I was in his life and happy he had found me.

On the night of the 'sofa conversation', I cried when he left. To me, he was letting me down gently, telling me to go out and find a long-term boyfriend and that he was just an interim. But after a few days of thinking about what he said, I realised that he was just being honest with me. He had never pretended that he had wanted me as his girlfriend. He wanted me to see what I had with him for what it was – a pure, utterly sexy interaction that could be enjoyed for now, for the moment. In one way, you could argue that he was being selfless, since he would know that I would probably start looking elsewhere.

And he was right. I did want more than just a sexual relationship. I didn't want to re-marry, and I certainly didn't want to live with another man after my husband's financial disasters. I didn't even want to be included in Blue's friends' lives or meet them. But I did want him to love me, and he clearly didn't.

He'd had a girlfriend two years earlier, whom he had loved. It was a difficult family situation into which he had integrated himself. She'd had three children by three different men, and each of the fathers still visited her house regularly to see their offspring. He said he would sometimes sit in the lounge while these men visited, occasionally at the same time as each other, and was unable to stop himself thinking that these men had had sex with his girlfriend. He tolerated this situation for a year and a half because he loved her. After six months, she had decided against any more sex but he stayed with her another year, hoping she would change her mind. That relationship, he said, had convinced him that conventional relationships were not for him. He had felt trapped and resentful that she had denied him sex for so long.

Here was I allowing him to sodomise me and spank me harder than I wanted, just so that I could be with him. And he couldn't love me. It wasn't his fault. That was life. You can't make yourself love someone if you don't. And you can't make someone love you if they don't. The more you try, the more likely they are to be pushed away and irritated.

I wasn't convinced that he couldn't fall in love. He had loved once, so he could love again, and it wouldn't be me. I asked once, nonchalantly, what would happen if he met a 40-year-old woman who didn't want kids, didn't want marriage, didn't want to live with him, but did want to be spanked. Would he go after her? He didn't hesitate. 'Yes, I would.' Where would that leave me? Getting old, alone.

Blue's point would be that that can happen anyway. He knew

many couples who were miserable together but stayed living together out of guilt, or financial reasons, or fear of being alone. Which is worse, he would ask me, in one of our 'relationship bollocks' (as he called it) conversations – being happy alone, able to see friends and lovers when you and they wanted, or being trapped in a relationship, and a house, that made you miserable? He argued that 'even if I loved you now, how long would that last?'

I did see Blue's point of view and he might well have been right in some aspects. Many couples split up. Many couples remain together without love. But sometimes relationships *do* work. In fact, relationships often work. And I was going to try and find one.

A seemingly minor issue, but one that was actually quite important to me, was the issue of holidays. Blue would never want to go on holiday with me, not for three days, or a week, or more. I was not going to spend the rest of my life either not going on holiday, going on holiday with other women, or going on holiday alone.

That night I knew I had to move on. It made me feel sad and empty, to think that, after six months, I would lose a lovely, funny guy with whom I had sometimes laughed so much that I had literally felt faint. But I needed to move on to someone who could eventually love me. I turned to the dating site that I had tried a few months before.

*****

I continued to see Blue, without telling him that I was looking for men on the internet. I didn't think there was much point since nothing might come of it. Also, he had said we were having an interaction, not a relationship. What's more, he had almost encouraged me to go out looking for the 'real deal'.

We continued to play the roles of dom and sub, but I was finding it increasingly difficult to feel enthusiastic about any of it, now that it wasn't part of a real relationship. I couldn't take it seriously now either. I found saying 'Sir' to someone I had been laughing with as an equal only moments before harder and harder. One day I told Blue this. He looked at me seriously and said, 'In that case, we should stop this dom-sub role-play from now on. It will just undermine my role as your dom if you can't call me 'Sir'.'

One part of me immediately regretted telling him, as I felt I was letting him down, but another part of me recognised that I wasn't enjoying it anymore, and wasn't prepared to put my heart and soul into it.

'Why can't we just carry on as dom and sub, but I don't have to call you 'Sir'?' I asked. 'After all, it's just a word.'

He fixed me with a grim stare. 'If it's just a word, why can't you use it?'

'I feel a bit silly saying it to you,' I admitted.

'Well, that's fine. We won't do it anymore,' he said matter-of-factly.

'I suppose I could try again,' I said, without much conviction.

'No, now that I know you don't like calling me 'Sir', I know that you've not properly entered into the spirit of being a submissive. I'd rather not continue with you as my sub.'

There was a long pause, and although I felt disappointed that I had failed as a sub again, I knew it was the right outcome for me. I *had* tried hard to be a good sub, but a part of me had been wondering for some time whether being so submissive that I was willing to lie on my back, legs apart, while someone whipped my buttocks and caressed my anus and vagina with a riding crop, would eat into my confidence, and start affecting me as a person in society. I had been mildly bullied by three people as I was growing up – an older sister, neighbour, and father. Although this current situation of being willingly controlled and 'bullied' by my dom was consenting play-acting, I had traits of personality that made me try to please too much, that wanted always to be accepted. I began to think that I was probably too likely to let this dominance, fun and sexy as I did often find it, seep into my 'normal' psyche.

I really just wanted Blue as a normal boyfriend, with a bit of spanking, and normal sex thrown in. To keep him, I had been willing to venture out of my comfort zone, but I knew inside it didn't feel right. We both had our own reasons not to want to continue, and both were valid. I also knew that he wasn't going to change, not for me, not for anyone. Blue was Blue, a free spirit.

'Are you disappointed?' I asked him. His answer surprised me.

'No, not disappointed. It's not a big thing with me. We can just carry on spanking and having sex without the role-play.'

Oh! Well, that was OK then. I wasn't going to lose him completely after all. And then he smiled wickedly at me. 'I can still dominate you, you know.'

Months later, we laughed about this conversation. He claimed I resigned as his sub. I claimed he fired me. I suppose it's a bit of both. He maintained I was still the worst sub he'd ever had, albeit a superb spankee.

He told me about a woman who had been his sub for about eight years before he knew me. She had been a 'real sub, not a pretend one' like me. He had spanked her so regularly that her bottom was nearly always sore. Apparently, as he started spanking her, the bruises would start appearing very quickly. I asked if she ever complained about the pain of the spankings. He said she often wriggled when she was over his knee and complained he was spanking too hard, but he continued anyway, knowing she could take more, and ensuring his dominance over her. She was a top corporate executive, at the head of a big company, and often had to chair large board meetings. She told him she loved sitting there, with a very sore bottom after he had thrashed her, knowing no one would suspect it of her.

So it was clearly not an issue for her, being a dominated, sometimes humiliated, sub one moment, and then switching the same day to a position of authority and decision-making. I wondered which was the real her. Did she long for someone to dominate her all the time, if she hadn't needed the job? Or was she really just a dominant, natural businesswoman, who like to play submissive for the sexual excitement?

A few days after the official dissolution of the dom-sub contract between Blue and me, I decided I needed a break from him to wipe the slate clean, so I could concentrate on two guys I had met on the dating sites. I wrote him an email explaining my reasons and truthfully telling him that I would miss him. He later told me that he had been quite upset to receive the email. His reply made me laugh, as usual. Part of it read, verbatim:

'And what I will always tell you is that, although I will never be the 'real deal', I spend time with you because I very much like you and enjoy your company, and I do the things that I do with you because I very much enjoy doing them with you. Is that really such a shitty deal for somebody, Anna? Does there have to be some well-constructed endgame to make something have a value and a worth? The endgame is that we're all going to die, so if you find somebody in your life whose company you enjoy, why keep pawing over the interaction that you have with them? Why not just enjoy it?

Now, I'm not suggesting you should prioritise such an interaction over the business of finding somebody to be miserable with for the rest of your life. You shouldn't, and you're right to be pursuing these online options. All I'm saying is that if you do, at some point, come back to what we have, please, please, please will you embrace it for everything that it offers, and stop fretting about what it doesn't offer, or thinking that it should somehow offer something more? Let it be what it is – you might enjoy it more! And it's not as though you can't then investigate other options, is it, as this current scenario ably illustrates.

So, yes, cheerio, at least for now – I will miss you too! And the very best of luck in your search for the 'real deal'.

P.S. Although I'll always be willing to 'take you back,' you should know that any or every time you return to me after a caper like this, your arse is going to be in for one helluva session, as punishment for the inconvenience you will have caused me by your absence!

PPS. Remember during these dating shenanigans that your anus remains my exclusive property, and is the pleasure of my cock only!'

After a few months, I got back in touch with Blue, but I only wanted to be friends this time. We continued to see each other on this basis for a year or two, and even had the occasional spanking, caning and belting session just for fun. There was no sex, even though Blue hoped I would relent (which I didn't). I continued to whinge a lot, but I needed the spankings to help maintain a thicker skin on my buttocks, so that I could more easily endure canings from clients. Blue and I still went out for meals, went to the cinema, and still made each other laugh, especially playing badminton. And even better was the fact that we would never have to end the relationship with each other because there wasn't one.

Chapter 10

Boyfriends and Babies

I thought about how I had reached this moment in my life. No boyfriend, no husband, no children, and not as much money as I would have liked. Age 57. I was still employed as a software developer, but the £20,000 debt my husband had landed on my plate still needed to be paid off, and every month a big chunk of my earnings went towards it.

My only goal in life had been to be married and have two children. I also assumed that I might be able to give up working to look after my two beautiful children. They would be a boy and a girl. The girl, Bethany, would be born first, and the boy, Ben, would be born two years later.

I never wanted to work anyway. I had zero ambition and didn't know what sort of career I wanted. It wouldn't be necessary because, at twenty years of age I was going to meet my future husband, and he would be the main breadwinner. I had a vague idea that, if I had to work, I would try being an air hostess. Then one day, I saw a programme where aspiring air hostesses and stewards were being trained to stand in front of a plane-load of passengers, make announcements over the intercom and go through the safety drills. I was exceptionally shy at that time and dreaded public speaking, especially in front of men, so decided to give that idea a miss.

*****

Boyfriends came and went. Four of them asked me to marry them, but they were never quite right. I became pregnant by two boyfriends but elected to terminate both pregnancies because I didn't love one of the fathers, and the other father was in the middle of trying to terminate me from the relationship. I didn't want to bring children into an unhappy home. I didn't know then what was to befall me.

Years later, I met my husband, aged thirty-seven. I decided to go on the pill as we were not ready for kids straight away. The first month I took the pill, my periods stopped – and never returned. I'll never forget the phone conversation I had the day I rang up for the results of a routine blood test. The day my life stood still.

'Hi. I'm just ringing up for my blood results.'

There was a pause while the nurse found the test results and came back to the phone. 'Ah yes. You're post-menopausal.'

It was as if she were telling me I had a cold and nothing to worry about. My world came down. The only goal I'd had for my entire life had just evaporated.

'But I'm thirty-nine. And I wanted children,' I managed to stammer down the phone.

The nurse suddenly seemed to realise the enormity of the news she had just imparted. 'Oohh. I'm sure the doctor will want to talk to you about this.'

I was beyond devastated. I would never be congratulated for having just had a baby. I would never breastfeed. Never build a sandcastle with my two-year-old. Never be the bride's mother and never have grandchildren. All the vital events in life that meant anything at all, as far as I was concerned, had just been snatched from my future.

The doctor was apologetic that I had heard the news so bluntly over the phone, but it didn't change the end result. He said he wondered if it had been a mistake, since I was so young. He asked me if I was still getting hot flushes and, as it happened, I hadn't had any for two weeks. 'Go home and make love,' he told me. 'There's a chance there's an egg that's just been released.'

I felt a stab of hope, but before I left the surgery, he warned me matter-of-factly, 'It won't happen again.'

Although I didn't see how he could possibly know it was the last egg (he turned out to be right), I was deflated by this last remark but still hopeful that I might yet create that longed-for child.

I went home and told Pen, who was less than enthusiastic.

'But I'm not ready. I want to travel more and jump and dive more with you.' We were both skydivers and scuba divers. 'We don't have the money to raise a child now.'

But I was desperate. 'This might be my very last chance to have my own child,' I virtually wailed at him.

We went for a walk to discuss it, and when I turned to look at him at one point, I saw a very anxious, reluctant, almost furious expression.

By the time we got home, however, I had somehow persuaded him to go upstairs with me and have sex. He took some time to climax and it was strangely louder than normal. I had my suspicions that he faked it to appease me, but I didn't challenge him as he would only have lied. After he got up from the bed and went downstairs, still disgruntled, I turned round, lay on my back and placed my feet up on the wall as far as they would go, to help the imagined sperm on their miraculous journeys through the womb and into the fallopian tubes, where my first-born would be conceived.

But I didn't become pregnant, and there never were any more eggs, at least not from the hot flushes that continued to rage through my body. Because I was so young to have the menopause, I was put on HRT (hormone replacement therapy) of combined oestrogen and progesterone to preserve my heart and bones. The hot flushes stopped, my libido returned to a luscious level, and my skin blossomed. I must admit that no periods from this early age for such a sporty girl was an unexpected bonus, but I would have suffered a lifetime of inconvenient monthly bleeds to have my own child at the right time with the right man.

And so followed, over about ten years, eight IVF cycles, all unsuccessful, each taking an emotional toll on us and our marriage – not to mention the huge financial burden. The £18,000 cost was all paid for by me, since Pen hardly had a penny to his name.

We then tried surrogacy and sent off a cheque for £600 for membership of 'Surrogacy UK'. A search for a surrogate mother was about to be set in motion. We'd had our first invitation to a meeting where 'intended parents', as they are called, can meet potential surrogates. We were delighted and secretly dreading it, since we were pretty sure we would be the oldest would-be parents there, and no surrogate would want to give her baby to a pair of oldies.

We never went to the meeting.

Pen died just after the invitation arrived. I had to ring the organisation to give them the news, asking if I could possibly go alone to the meeting. The girl I spoke to sounded genuinely shocked since I'd been talking to her excitedly the previous week. She had to tell me that, unfortunately, they couldn't allow a baby to be given to a single parent, and they would be returning my £600.

Chapter 11

Spanking Parties

I had often wondered about spanking parties without really wanting to take part. My sister had once told me that a shy colleague of hers confided in her that she went to spanking parties. The colleague had looked sheepish and embarrassed when describing how she had bent over an armchair in front of everyone with her skirt up and knickers down. My sister merely remarked how brave her colleague was to have admitted such a thing to her. I was secretly fascinated but didn't want to admit it to my sister, who is religious and might not have approved of my interest.

Jeremy, who regularly organises parties, explained there was a thriving commercial party scene in England, mainly in London and The Midlands. Commercial parties are where participating ladies receive payment in the form of a financial gift, which is usually an amount recommended by the organiser.

Although this means by definition that there is a financial relationship between players, ladies who are invited almost always have a natural predisposition or inclination towards the pleasures of spanking. This gives them the best of both worlds – enjoyable spankings (whether giving or receiving) and a generous financial reward.

(Jeremy told me that non-commercial parties also exist, where no money exchanges hands, and apparently there is a thriving community of this type too, but he had no experience of these.)

Larger parties generally take place in hired venues such as pub function rooms, night clubs or swingers' clubs. Smaller parties are usually organised in private houses. The ratio of men to women is an important consideration and can vary considerably. Ratios of 3/1, 4/1 or higher are quite common, but the more exclusive and elite parties aim for as close to 2/1 as possible.

After some general socialising, the exact format of a commercial spanking party will vary from organiser to organiser but invariably it will be structured around three traditional rounds of over-the-knee spanking, implements and caning.

The over-the-knee round is usually conducted with all the men sitting in a circle. All the girls go over their knees, moving round the circle one by one. Their skirts may be lifted up and knickers taken down with each encounter, then raised back up at the end of each spanking so they can get up and walk on with dignity to the next man. The girls are usually not nude above the waist.

For the implements and caning rounds, which seem to be the pinnacle of the party, the men are usually divided into groups. One girl is assigned to each group to be dealt with by each guy in turn before she moves on to the next group.

Typically, each girl, in turn, walks over to a chair or bench, lifts up her own skirt, takes down her knickers (or has them taken down) in front of everyone and bends over. Each man, in turn, will then give her six strokes of an implement or cane. This is not with excessive force, but enough to sting and leave a few red marks – 'party level' as it's called.

It is no small challenge in front of an audience to deliver six accurate strokes of the cane, and for this reason, out of respect to both caner and canee, Jeremy will ask for quiet while caning is in progress. Once the sixth stroke has successfully been delivered, however, the audience is encouraged to applaud.

At smaller parties, the approach tends to be more tailored to individual needs. Jeremy, who pre-pandemic had been running highly-structured and personalised parties for more than ten years, gave me an outline of his approach:

'My aim is to provide a relaxed and friendly atmosphere at levels with which everyone is comfortable. The safety and well-being of the girls are of paramount importance, and as such, personal dignity and limits will always be respected. The standard party size is nine guys and four girls, although this may vary slightly depending on bookings. Larger parties, such as New Year's Eve and the Summer Special, extend to a maximum of twelve guys and six girls. There are the three traditional rounds of OTK, implements and caning but with a lot more besides, such as games, tutorials and girl on girl spanking. A key feature is that each guy will have the opportunity for a private mini 121 wherein, if he chooses, switching may be included. A quality buffet meal is served halfway through the proceedings, and for those who want to stay on into the evening to enjoy further social interaction with like-minded people, there is an optional meal at a local restaurant.'

I wanted to be a fly on the wall.

Jeremy did, on occasion, offer me the opportunity to take part in a spanking party, either as a spankee or as a hostess where I would only be helping to serve food, or organise the drinks, while being allowed to watch the proceedings from a safe distance to gauge if I wanted to join in either then or at a later party.

I did think about it but declined. I was fifty-eight and thought my body would not to match up with those of the younger girls, however sporty I was. You can't really beat youth. I wasn't convinced either that my current tolerance had reached party level.

I also didn't want to show other girls my vagina. What if theirs were neater than mine? I hadn't had any complaints or comments from men but perhaps that was out of politeness, and they probably didn't mind or care or notice anyway. In fact, experienced spankers and spankees have probably seen such a variety of vaginas over the years that nothing would surprise them now.

When I told Jeremy these reasons, he sent me a very kind email, the main section of which is shown verbatim below:

'As for a party, rest assured I wouldn't invite you if I did not

think it was suitable for you, or if I didn't think you would fit in, or if I thought it was beyond your limits. On the whole, levels of play at my parties are less exacting than 121s. It's true that the OTK rounds(s) are quite intense, but I carefully moderate the use of implements and cane. You should have no worries about being outclassed in looks and remember you are only ever naked below the waist. Looks-wise, the main focus of the guys' attention will be your bottom, and believe me, you can take 'pride' in that part of your anatomy.'

But I didn't relish the idea of a roomful of people watching me take my knickers down and take a caning. Apart from other girls seeing my vagina, what if the whole affair turned me on and I started lubricating so much that it became visible?

I did, however, accept an invitation to Jeremy's house to have a different type of session from just a 121 with him. He was sensitive to my dislike of group activity so he had invited one other guy and one other girl. I didn't mind about the other guy being there, but I wasn't sure about having another girl there. What if she was about twenty and unfriendly?

I arrived first and helped Jeremy prepare lunch. The second guy, Stan, arrived soon after and I immediately felt at ease with him. He was one of the friendliest guys you could hope to meet. Over lunch, he told us about a caning session he had requested for himself from a mistress (as women are called who are paid to cane others) as a punishment he felt he deserved for some misdemeanour. He said he'd taken seventy-two hard strokes of the cane on his back and bottom, and felt cleansed afterwards. I couldn't imagine the bruises his body must have sustained, and I wondered what he'd done to think he deserved such punishment. But I didn't ask, and he didn't offer an explanation.

I had a 121 with Stan in one of the upstairs bedrooms as soon as lunch was over, while Jeremy did the washing up downstairs. I wondered if he could hear the slaps. Stan soon had me naked and spanked me quite hard over his knee. He chatted amicably throughout the spanking and never went into domineering spanker mode. He kept asking if I was OK and if the severity wasn't too much for me to bear.

We tried several different implements, and he then caned me about ten to fifteen times as I lay over the bed. It hurt, but the thicker layer of skin on my bottom by then allowed me to take it without too many yelps.

Then I heard the doorbell ring. I was really nervous about meeting a fellow spankee, but I needn't have worried. Laura was a lovely, friendly, down-to-earth girl, aged about forty. She immediately went upstairs to one of the allocated bedrooms to change into her spankee attire, namely an ordinary skirt that could be easily raised. When I'd finished with Stan, I joined her in the bedroom to change into a dress. She chatted away quite happily. She told me there was a strong, sisterly sentiment among the spankees and never any bitchiness. She'd been a spankee for several years, so knew the scene and its members well.

Jeremy called us all downstairs into the lounge. He asked Laura and me to bend over two chairs with our elbows resting on the chairs, our backs arched, our legs straight and feet apart. Apparently, new spankees often round their backs rather than arch them, which doesn't present their bottoms for spanking as nicely. He told us both to raise our skirts onto our backs. Then he walked over to Laura and pulled her knickers down. I heard another set of footsteps and realised Stan was standing behind me. I felt my knickers being taken down to my knees. I looked across at Laura bending over the other chair, in the same position as me, elbows on the chair's seat. She was grinning. I was beginning to enjoy myself too.

Stan spanked me with his hand for a few minutes, and then he and Jeremy swapped over and I was spanked by hand by Jeremy while Stan spanked Laura. Then we moved to the sofa and armchair respectively and had an OTK session with each man in turn.

At one point, I looked across the room at Stan as he spanked

Laura over his knee as she lay longways across the sofa. Her bottom was bare and reddening, her knickers round her knees. They were chatting away to each other like old friends and clearly having a good time. At one point, they were talking about shopping for different vegetables, and there didn't seem to be any attempt to create a scenario of punishment or discipline between the two. In a way, I felt something was missing. It was the middle of the afternoon, the sitting room was lit by ordinary sunlight, and we could well have been having a simple tea party for all the merry chit-chat and friendly banter that was taking place.

I suppose in a group situation it was harder to role-play and take a scenario of punishment seriously, as the atmosphere was so jovial. But also Stan and Laura had been explicitly invited by Jeremy to introduce me to the party scene in a gentle and non-threatening way, and this goal was very much being achieved. This was an excellent way for me to see the fun that could be experienced. I appreciated Jeremy's kind efforts to organise this mini spanking party for me, as well as Stan and Laura's time in taking part for my sake. It must have been rather tame from their point of view, but I got the feeling the spanking community looks out for its own members.

Then Jeremy said he wanted to show me an example of a party caning, but didn't expect me to participate. He asked Laura to walk over to the caning bench at the side of the lounge, raise her skirt, pull down her own knickers and bend over the bench while we watched. A slightly more serious atmosphere descended on our group of four.

The bench Jeremy used on this occasion consisted of a triangular wooden structure about three feet high, like the legs of a trestle table without the tabletop. Across the top was a padded, leather cushion for the spankee to bend over. A chaise longue or armchair could also be used.

Stan took up position with the cane while I watched from the safety of one of the armchairs. Jeremy reminded everyone that this was the part that was to be taken seriously. Jokey comments, as in a normal spanking party, at this point would be silenced. Comments about the woman's anatomy were especially forbidden.

Stan showed Laura the cane he was going to use, but she decided she wanted another one. Jeremy whispered to me that this was called 'topping from the bottom' – where the spankee is in fact in control of proceedings by strength of character.

Stan gave her five light strokes of the cane as a demonstration for me, making her count each one. 'One, thank you, Sir. Two, thank you, Sir.'

'And what do we say about the last one, young lady?'

'It's the hardest,' giggled Laura. The cane came up, swished through the air, and landed on Laura's bottom with a gentle thwack, only slightly harder than the other five strokes.

'Six, thank you, Sir.'

Laura got up off the caning bench, still smiling. Even though an atmosphere of punishment was still lacking, it was fascinating to see someone else being caned. Not something you see in your lounge every day. I asked Laura if it had hurt her, and she said simply, with a smile, 'No'. She had been in the spanking business for years, so the skin on her bottom must have been nicely thickened by then.

Then Laura and Stan disappeared into a bedroom for a 121 while Jeremy and I adjourned to the playing room. He had placed a piece of A4 paper with a letter typed on it in the middle of the desk. He told me to bend over the desk so that my face was about a foot from the letter.

'Now Miss Skye. Read the letter out loud – and slowly,' he ordered.

I began reading.

'More slowly.'

I slowed down. I reached a word that was spelt wrong and wondered if Jeremy realised. I didn't have to wonder for long. A sharp spank over my skirt as I read it out told me he was fully aware of the spelling.

'That word is spelt wrong, Miss Skye. You will have to retype it.

Carry on reading.'

I read out the next sentence, where there were no mistakes. I felt Jeremy behind me, ready to pounce. I could see a misspelled word coming up in the next sentence. As I reached the misspelled word, I braced myself for the next punishment. And it duly came.

Wallop!

'Another mistake. Retype that one as well!' He raised my skirt and the tirade continued over my knickers, and then on my bare bottom.

In the middle of this session, Laura knocked on the door to say her goodbyes. I was bent over the desk with my bottom on full display facing the door as she walked in, but she didn't bat an eyelid. She walked up to me, gave me a big hug and said she hoped I would enjoy the rest of the day. I was sorry to see her go. As the only other spankee I had ever met, I felt quite an affinity with her.

With the door open, Jeremy called Stan into the room. Then followed one of the sexiest moments of my life. I was stripped naked. Jeremy placed a chair in the middle of the room and pulled me over his lap. He started spanking my already red bottom on the buttock nearest him and encouraged Stan to start spanking my other buttock at the same time. They quickly fell into a rhythm whereby their hands spanked alternately. So there I was, completely naked in front of two men, being spanked by both of them at the same time. The spanking lasted only three or four minutes, but I will remember it for the rest of my life.

When the session was over, Jeremy called me into the lounge, where he gave me tea and biscuits. He had set up the film *The Secretary* at a certain scene that he thought I might now find familiar. I watched with amusement as the girl in the movie went through the same spanking scene with the typed letter that I had just endured. I told him I had found the session *very* sexy. I also appreciated his efforts to think up such a scenario.

I then had another 121 session with Stan. He suggested that we first go outside into the garden and use the bench, where he could warm me up in preparation for the caning he was planning to give me later in the bedroom. He asked me to kneel on the bench, facing away from him, and raise my skirt. He had brought with him a leather paddle and proceeded to wallop me with relish. I wondered if the people on the bowling green could hear the strokes so I tried not to let any sound pass my lips. Jeremy was watching this activity with amusement from the house and decided to take the photo below. When he sent me the photo later, he emphasised that photography is not normally allowed at parties to preserve the identity and confidentiality of the participants.

Stan and I in Jeremy's garden, using a leather paddle to prepare me for my later caning by him. It should be noted that I wasn't presenting my bottom for Stan as well as I learnt to later for other clients. My back is slightly hunched, rather than arched, but Stan was too polite to correct my posture at the time. I recently asked Jeremy what the official name of the implement was, and this was his full, enthusiastic and eloquent reply:

"I rescued this particular implement from the waste bin at a party over a decade ago. It had been thrown away after the stitching at the

base of the handle had come adrift.

It's amazing what can be achieved with a short strip of black insulating tape and I am happy to say it is still in active service all these years later. Apart from being a personal favourite, it is regularly selected as the implement of choice at my parties.

Best described as a flexible, double-layered, soft leather lollipop paddle. Accurate and skilful delivery rewards the spanker with a most satisfying 'smacking' sound, whilst simultaneously imbuing the spankee with a warm, glowing suffusion of delight across a wider surface area. Its admirable effects are clearly evident in the photograph.

As a warm-up implement, it was a perfect match for your bottom." [Photo by Russell de Mille.]

Stan and I then adjourned to one of the bedrooms. He told me to bend over the side of the bed then used a light bamboo cane to give me ten fairly hard strokes. This time I didn't hold back from giving a few quiet yelps. I decided to ask him if I looked as if I was turned on. He immediately felt my wet lips with his fingers and told me he thought I definitely was. He must have taken my previous enquiry as an invitation. He suddenly asked me if I could tweak his nipples. I said I'd rather not, but he begged me to do it just for a while, so I relented, reluctantly, so as not to ruin the atmosphere. I grasped his right nipple and pulled at it rather aimlessly. What are you supposed to do with a nipple? Do you yank it or twist it? Both sound rather painful. Then suddenly I felt his lips between my legs. He had decided to go down on me without asking my permission or warning me. I wasn't pleased and, after a few seconds, I asked him to stop, which he did immediately. We dressed quickly after that, in embarrassed silence, and went downstairs to the relative safety of Jeremy.

Stan reckoned I'd had enough of being spanked and caned by then as my bottom was very purple. But I had promised another session with Jeremy in return for all the food and drink he'd provided and didn't want to renege on an agreement. So I had yet another session with Jeremy that day.

We went into his bedroom, and I noticed that, as once before, there were several mirrors placed around the room. This allowed me to watch myself being spanked, belted and caned. It opened up another dimension to the session for me since the spankee is normally rather restricted to watching the floor and the man's feet and cannot anticipate when the strokes are going to land. With the mirrors, I was able to see the best position to place my back and bottom for presentation and could also brace myself for the impending punishment.

By the end of the day, my bottom was feeling very sore. Both spankers had used the cane in their two respective sessions with me. I had taken over 100 strokes of the cane throughout the day – I know because I had been made to count many of them as usual. I was paid £150 by Stan and £30 petrol expenses by Jeremy, who had the spanking sessions with me free of charge, by prior arrangement, since he had provided food and drink, the accommodation, and done all the organisation. Apart from the occasional over-enthusiastic stroke of the cane and the nipple event, I had enjoyed every minute.

'No need to worry about your level of tolerance now,' Jeremy commented as I left.

The following week all the colours of the rainbow appeared on my bottom – I likened it to the Northern Lights in a text to Jeremy – but I just felt proud of myself. With Jeremy's reassurance, I reckoned I had indeed turned from rookie spankee to party-level spankee.

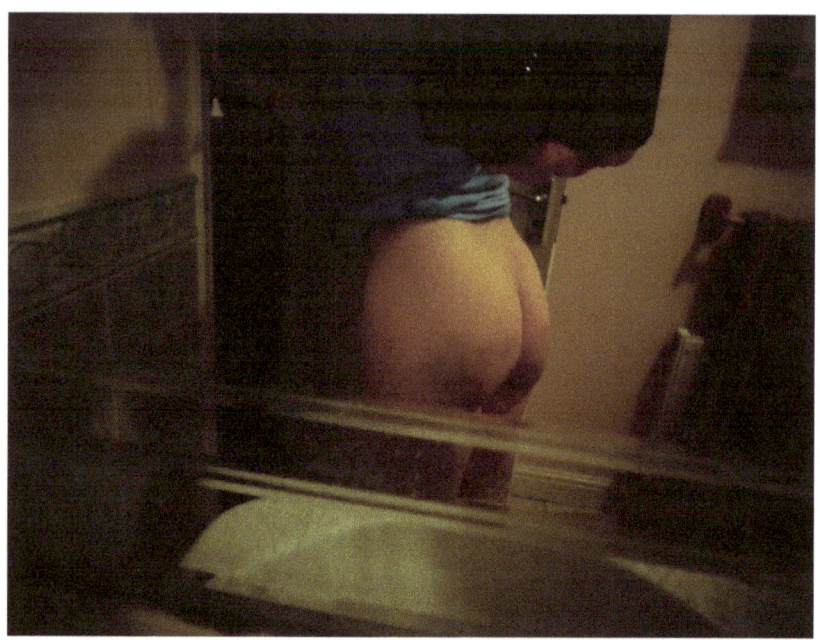

After my session with Stan and Jeremy. Note the accuracy of the strokes by these two experienced spankers, always landing on the lower half of the buttocks.

Chapter 12

The Problem with Novices

One of the issues of new spankers is that they might not quite 'get' the whole CP concept. Even though none of the men I had met for spanking had turned out to be dangerous, I felt I had to vet them quite carefully, particularly if they appeared new to the scene. Vanilla people often seemed to think the spanking scene is all about pain and domination, without grasping the idea that it should all be consensual fun.

I had heard of a novice spanker who had used a cane that seemed to be made partly of metal on a spankee. It was only after the ferocity of the first stroke that she realised it was no ordinary cane. She managed to escape but was extremely bruised.

I mainly used the opening emails they sent me to accept or reject them. If it was a one-liner, I tended to answer that I wasn't available. It tended to show that they were completely unaware of how the CP world worked. Two examples (verbatim):

'Can we use my car so u can so I can spank u.' Er – I don't think so.
'Hey, wanna talk U reply if u read this mail.' No, thank you.

If their spelling and grammar were good, and it was basically a civilised letter, treating me as if I were a human being, I replied positively.

One such email read:

'I am going to be in Taunton in a couple of weeks' time and wondered whether you might be around that sort of area. You could come along to my hotel

where I am staying and we could then if you wanted have dinner together either before or after playing. Hope to hear back from you.'

(I wasn't in that area, so we never met up.)

*****

One young man started off in an acceptable manner:

'Hi saw your ad on the site you look perfect, I am 23 years old 6ft tall and live in market Drayton shropshire, I love giving a good spanking and you seem like you like receiving a good spanking. How hard can I spank U? How good is your pain barrier? I like to give a good hard spanking but need to no you would be able to take it? What may I get to spank?'

His grammar was slightly dubious, but I gave him the benefit of the doubt, and replied that he could only spank my bottom, clothed or naked, with hand, belt, strap, slipper, flip flop, riding crop and paddle, and that my pain barrier was not bad, I'd been told. His next reply led me to reject him. He *was* only asking about sex, but I had to be careful, especially as I thought it unlikely a 23-year-old with that level of grammar and spelling would have the sort of money he quoted:

'Wow that sounds good to me ;) so is what has been talked about the only kind of service provided by you? If not id like to hear more, and do u travel? Getting to you isnt an issue just work ect be easier if you came to me? Your sounding perfect so far and I have £5000 to spend so what would that get me from you?'

*****

One guy, who I will call Frank, since we met at the Frankley Services on the M5, contacted me via the website, where it clearly stated I was available to be spanked, not provide sexual favours.

He was about 6'4" and seemed quite pleasant as we made

conversation over a cup of tea in the Services café. He asked about what he could and couldn't do with me, and seemed pleased with the answers. Then his attitude subtly changed.

'And what will you do for me?' he said pointedly.

'Ah. I'm afraid I'm there just to be spanked. Not to give sexual favours.'

'I see. So you get all the fun, and I do all the work,' he said. His demeanour had become slightly aggressive.

'Well, hopefully you will enjoy spanking me, and touching me,' I said, relieved that we were in a crowded café and not already in a hotel room. I decided there and then that I wouldn't be meeting him for any subsequent spanking session.

'That doesn't seem fair. I think you should reconsider your terms and give something back.'

When I emphasised that it didn't work like that, he said he wasn't interested and got up to leave. I followed him out into the car park, and we just about managed a terse goodbye before going our separate ways.

About a week later, I received an email from Frank saying he was sorry that he'd asked me for sex and that he'd misunderstood the concept. He had looked into the spanking world's 'rules' and contacted a few other spankees and they had all confirmed the accepted approach. Now that he understood that a spankee is just that – there to be spanked – would I like to meet him for a spanking session? No thanks. I thought it was nice of him to apologise and admit his mistake, but who knows where his tendency for aggression might have led, had it been just myself and him, a man of 6' 4", in a hotel room, with no witnesses.

*****

One man kept emailing me from Lancashire for months before being brave enough to come and meet me. He said he had wanted to spank for years and years but never had the courage. We arranged to meet near some fields near me, where I hoped to find a log or fence that I could bend over. I parked my car near some shops in a village and almost immediately received a text to say he had seen me arrive and was coming over to the car. It felt as if we were on a blind date.

I slid out of the car and saw a small (about 5'4"), young guy walking towards me, smiling and waving. After the preliminary niceties, we quickly decided to try and look for a fence in a nearby field, away from prying eyes. We walked down the road and out of the village, chatting about his journey down, and his spanking ideas. Within a minute or two, we came across a small field with no houses or sheds in sight. It did indeed have a style into it, with a convenient wooden pole across the top. He agreed that I should bend over the style, but I noticed he no longer looked too sure of the situation.

I was wearing a short black skirt, black tights, and black boots. I waited a second or two, without looking round at him, to give him the time to believe that the moment he'd been waiting many years for had finally arrived. I felt him slowly raise my skirt, then pull down my knickers, then he gave me two or three gentle slaps on my bare bottom with his hand. Then he stopped.

'Sorry but I can't do this. I feel silly.'

'Oh, okay,' I said, trying to lessen his embarrassment. 'That's fine. We can go back to the hotel if you like. Perhaps it will feel more conducive to spanking there.' He readily agreed.

We got to the hotel room, and I suggested I put myself over his knee over the bed. The same thing happened. After wanting to spank someone for years and sending me many long emails about his fetish, when confronted with the reality of it, he suddenly couldn't go through with it. He then admitted that it was partly just an excuse to get me naked and feel my body, as he didn't have much success with women. I didn't mind at all. I undressed in front of him and put myself across the bed on my back. He lay beside me and began gently feeling my body and massaging my breasts and vagina. He didn't seem to expect anything in return, and I didn't offer anything. I was continually surprised that men allowed this situation, where I got all the fun, and didn't offer anything in return, except my body. He had been honest with me, and I was glad to help him.

When he returned home, he started writing copious emails again, about how he'd enjoyed meeting me and how he would definitely spank me the next time we met. I wondered if there'd be a next time since Lancashire was a fair distance. I also doubted he'd be any braver the second time. When he asked me if I'd like to see a photo of his penis, even in fun, I stopped the communication. I didn't want him to get the wrong idea about my intentions. I was only interested in spanking and only allowed the occasional hand straying out of politeness. I tried never to encourage it, especially not in the lead-up to a spanking session.

Chapter 13

Fetishes

'Hello Lily-Rose,
this is The Master of the Estate here otherwise known as Charles, I have received reports about you in connection with unsatisfactory and inapropriate behaviour, therefore I must inform you that you are required to report to the manor so we can discuss the the consequences of your actions. You are herby notified that you must forward your phone number to me so we can discuss a time and date for your appointment and discuss the necessary chastisement.
A prompt reply would be in your best interests.

Yours
Charles X
(Master of the Estate)'

I received the above email (verbatim, apart from disguised names) when I was starting to get used to the sort of requests and clients I wanted as a spankee. The term 'Master of the Estate' made me chuckle. He was obviously an experienced spanker, looking for some entertaining fun.

I replied in the same vein:

'Ha ha! Nice one.
Hi Your Worship,
Just to say - thanks for this order to report to you and be punished. I look forward to it. Oh I mean I am very worried about what you might do to me.
More about me - I don't switch. My rates are £70 for the first hour, £50 per hour after that pro rata. I will travel up to an hour to meet you. I have only

just started in the CP scene, don't take the cane, but do take other implements lightly. (Sorry!) Can be spanked to 'party level'. Will do total nudity and touching, but don't do sexual favours.

If this is of interest to you, I look forward to hearing from you.

Lily-Rose'

His reply came back immediately:

'Hello Lily-Rose,

thankyou for your prompt reply,very wise it saves you getting in deeper trouble.I look forward to meeting you in the near future, in the meantime it would be helpful if you could let me know where you live within a mile or so and suggest a convienient location to meet.It would be helpful an I'm sure pleasant if we could have a chat and it would also be easier to make arrangements for a meeting,to that end would you please let me have a phone number I can contact you on.To make matters easier you could always text me on ---------------- and say a convienient time to ring you.

Looking forward to a prompt reply.

Yours
Charles X (Master of the Estate)'

Soon after this exchange, we met for a coffee late one morning on a sunny day in a hotel near my home. I arrived at the hotel car park, and as I parked, I realised we didn't know the makes of each other's cars. I sat there for about ten minutes, and then saw in my side mirror a large, elderly man getting out of his car and walking towards me. He had also been sitting in his car, waiting. I got out of my car, and he waved at me, grinning.

Charles was a gentle giant, aged about 70, and well-spoken, as I was beginning to find that many of them were. As I suspected, he was very experienced and knew exactly what he wanted. He liked OTK – but also worryingly the use of a kitchen spatula. My heart sank at the thought of his using the spatula on me. It wasn't going to bend an inch, and I knew it was going to sting. I said I would try it but warned him that I might not like it. He wasn't bothered at all.

'That's absolutely fine. We'll just go back to OTK and then I will use the oils on you.'

'Oils? Is that some type of implement?'

'No,' he laughed, 'they are for me to rub all over your body. To soothe a sore bottom.'

I quite liked the sound of that.

During this initial face-to-face conversation, I decided that he was completely safe to bring back to my house. So started a series of sessions with the Master of the Estate that were really quite erotic. As soon as we got home, he ordered me over his knee. On this first encounter, I was wearing my usual short, yellow summer dress, white shoes, white knickers, and no bra as requested. The dress came up quickly and the knickers came down. It was just the warm-up of about ten slaps. Then he ordered me to stand up and take off all my clothes in front of him, as he sat on my sofa. There was no mention of the 'Master of the Estate' scenario. That seemed to be just in the email introduction.

I undressed and then had to stand in front of him so that he could gently play with my body. I never knew where to look when men did this. Should I look into his eyes? I decided to look straight ahead. I also didn't know what to do with my arms so I just let them hang down by my side. I wondered why men didn't mind the fact that I didn't touch them. Wasn't it frustrating for them? Perhaps they hoped I would change my mind if I was aroused enough.

He seemed too intent on my body to care where my eyes were looking or what my arms were doing. He slid his hand between my legs and the other hand played with my breasts. Then he suddenly picked me up and put me over his knee, where he spanked me much harder and for much longer than the warm-up. My bottom was beginning to sting.

'Go and fetch a spatula,' he ordered. 'Your bottom looks nice and warmed up.'

I went into the kitchen and fetched a spatula. As I came out of the kitchen completely naked, holding the spatula, he gazed at me.

'Just look at that,' he said with a smile, 'what a sight for sore eyes. A naked lady coming to be thrashed with a spatula by me.'

I tried to smile, but I was getting slightly concerned about the oncoming pain.

'Stand in front of me, and face sideways.'

I stood about a yard from him, with my left side facing him, in position for his right arm and the spatula to swing. He placed the spatula on my bottom, and then tapped my bottom gently with it.

'How was that?' he asked.

'Just about OK.'

He gave me three or four harder taps.

'Hmmm. Just about OK,' I said gingerly.

So then came three hard strokes, one after the other. They stung badly and I cried out.

'Not sure I can take any more,' I said, rather disappointed at my own tolerance.

'Well done. You took a lot,' he said, kindly. 'Now come here so I can feel your gorgeous body again. Spread your legs wide.'

After a few minutes, he declared that he was ready to rub oil all over me, and that it would be better on the bed. He had a sheet to lay over the bed to protect the covers from the oil.

We went upstairs and lay on the bed together; he was fully dressed while I was fully naked. I trusted him not to try anything other than rub the oils on me. He kept to his word. He rubbed several oils over my bottom and then all over my back, shoulders, arms and tummy. It was very sensual and did soothe me. He didn't ask for anything in return, and I didn't offer, although a few times I rubbed one of the oils on his back. I sometimes did feel selfish not giving anything sexual back, but spankers knew the rules before engaging with me. I stuck to the 'contract' between us and just let it be a one-way flow.

I saw Charles several times throughout my eighteen months as a spankee. The sessions always took the same format at my house and I never raised the fee above £70, although after a few months, he kindly asked whether I would like the normal £100 per hour. He always brought the oils and I began to look forward to their fragrance and soothing sensation. He continued to demand the spatula but as I continued to complain, he used it more and more sparingly until most of the sessions were just OTK and oils.

*****

I came across some other strange fetishes during my first year as a spankee. I received the following very polite email from a spanker in Ireland:

'I hope you are well. I saw ur ad on the website. Im visiting UK next week exact date not settled yet its flexible depending on when ur free and so on. There is a very specific fantasy I want to act out and I'm seeing if you'd like to do it. Can I say at the outset apologies if u don't like the idea or I'm being too graphic.
Ok here goes ... The fantasy is as follows:
Girl wears a school uniform pleated skirt, shirt tie and jumper white socks and pink knickers.
Here's where it gets a little eccentric. I then want u to wet ur knickers and stand in front of me in the wet for about five minutes. Then say Daddy I've wet myself. I will ten give out to u for doing such and spank u with hand, belt and paddle then make u go in the corner.
Ok so that's it is it something you would/ could do. Anyway that's what I'm looking for thanks for reading and again I hope it was ok to be so direct.
Yours ... '

I surprised myself by accepting his invitation but said I would only be able to produce a few drops of urine and would definitely not be able to urinate fully in front of him. On that basis, he politely declined to meet me.

*****

One guy wanted to shave me, so I was paid to lie on the bathroom floor while he pasted turquoise shaving foam all over my labia and then proceeded to gently shave me. Actually, it was very soothing. He then made me wear a skimpy dominatrix suit and crawl on all fours round the room while he beat me with a spatula and a wooden spoon. It really hurt, and I didn't enjoy it. When I reached the door, I started turning round to begin the return crawl back across the room, but he ordered me to carry on in the same direction. 'Er – there's a door in my way,' I commented, but he insisted, 'Just keep going. Did I tell you to turn round?' So I had to pretend to crawl through the solid door. All about domination, not logic. Whatever floats your boat.

At the end of the session, I asked him if he wanted the dominatrix suit back.

'Ooh no thanks. You keep it. The wife would wonder why I had THAT in my car.'

*****

Another man tied my hands behind my back with metal handcuffs and blindfolded me, while I stood in his lounge completely naked and he played with my body. I found this very sexy. He had spanked me over his knee but then said he wanted to cane me with a big heavy cane. It was long, unbendable and just under half an inch thick (he kindly measured it for me later for the previous book). I said I didn't think I could take it, so he said he would do it quite gently. I took about twelve strokes of medium force without complaining too much.

'Can I just try one hard one?' he pleaded. I wanted to know what that would be like, so I agreed. After all, it would be over in a second. I didn't realise that the harder the stroke, the more likely it is that the cane will miss the right spot (the lower half of the bottom) and fall too high or too low, both of which can be very painful and give deep bruising.

He placed it on my buttocks and asked if I was ready. I said I was, and then I heard the swish of it through the air before it landed with a sickening thwack on the top half of my buttocks, missing the accepted target area of the more fleshy part. I shuddered with the agonising pain as it shot through my body. I let out a loud wailing howl and curled my hands up to my face in agony. He saw that it was way more than I could take, and put his arms round me, saying 'oh sorry, sorry. I won't do that again.'

The bruise that emerged was large, round, purple and black and blue, about two inches in diameter. It stayed for three or four weeks, and at one point I was actually worried it wasn't going to fade completely. I had to cancel three other spanking appointments, partly because spankers normally like a pure-as-the-driven-snow bottom to work on, but also because I couldn't bear the thought of anyone going near the bruise. But it wasn't the guy's fault. He had asked me, and I had said yes.

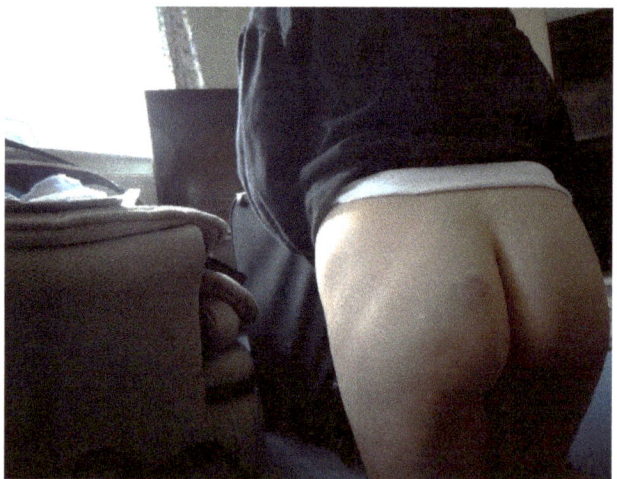

Two weeks after the stroke with the big heavy cane, the bruise was still showing. Rather proud of my achievement, I quickly took a photo before it subsided further. I wished I had snapped the bruise in its magnificent heyday. This is not to say that bruising spankees was the point of spanking. Far from it. It was only that I was proud of having proof that I had taken such punishment.

*****

One guy had asked me to wear a very short skirt to the session. When I walked into the hotel room, I noticed a number of sweets commonly known as 'opal fruits', scattered on the floor. He told me to bend down with straight legs apart and pick them up slowly while he watched from behind. He then ordered me to undress completely while he watched and told me to go and stand in front of the window, which looked out onto the street one floor below. He came over and stood very close behind me. He waited until there were people walking on the street below and then reached round and started to fondle both breasts. He ordered me to spread my legs. One hand then went down and he fondled my labia while the public walked by oblivious. He then ordered me onto the bed on all fours and whipped me with what he called a 'pipe', a bendy, fairly malleable round stick of white rubber or leather about two feet long. It looked more painful than it was.

He kept his 'piece de resistance' until the end. He ordered me to lie on my back on the bed in the diaper position, where he held me practically vertically by the ankles with one hand and whipped my bottom with the other using the pipe.

This same guy suddenly put on rubber gloves while I lay on the bed waiting for another spanking. I whirled round and asked what he was doing. 'Oh don't worry. I have a cut on my finger. I didn't want the blood to touch you while I feel your pussy.'

With the session over, and when I was fully dressed, we started chatting like friends as we left the hotel room. A bond often forms between spanker and spankee during and after a session.

'I have one request,' I said to him. He turned to look at me quizzically, almost bracing himself for some weird return fetish on my part.

'Can I keep the opal fruits?' They were still in my pocket from when I had picked them up earlier. He laughed, almost with relief, and said I could, with pleasure, keep them all.

*****

Another young and inexperienced spanker wanted me to sit on a space hopper in his lounge, naked from the waist down and face the corner. He ordered me to move backwards and forwards over the space hopper using my bottom only, so that my buttocks and rectum stuck out backwards towards him over the side of the hopper. He squatted down behind me and watched. Each to his own.

Later the same evening, after he had given me a belting over his bed and table, he suddenly disappeared from the bedroom and returned with cream on his middle finger.

'What are you going to do with that?' I asked, slightly concerned.

'I thought you would like this.' He indicated my bottom. Where on earth would he have got that notion from? Just because spankees like being spanked, it doesn't follow that we like having foreign objects inserted into our rectums.

'Er no. Sorry, I don't.'

'Oh. So sorry. I won't do it then.'

He never asked to see me again but later, he had the cheek to ask me to give him a good reference in case he wanted to see younger spankees.

Chapter 14

Canes, Crops, Slippers and Hairbrushes

Often during spanking sessions, especially at the beginning during the social chat, spanker and spankee exchange spanking stories. It's often the only time either can talk openly about their 'hobby' or 'career', since the wife won't hear of it, and friends might think you're strange or become embarrassed.

One spanker told me he'd had a previous session with a spankee who asked him to cane her. He started caning her with the usual amount of restraint, but she encouraged him to use more and more force. He noticed she was getting extremely aroused. He continued until her bottom was so covered with angry purple welts that he was afraid he would cause her to bleed so he refused to carry on, to her great disappointment.

How someone could take that amount of bodily pain and actually relish it, I will never know. It also begs the question why the men should always pay when we women do seem to enjoy it sometimes.

*****

One guy, who was sixty-five, just wanted to use the riding crop on me. When I first arrived at his room in the Holiday Inn, he made me stand in the middle of the room. 'Let's take a look at you.'

I was wearing a knee-length tight-fitting black dress and black high-heeled shoes. Underneath were stockings and suspenders, by his prior request.

He walked over to me, bent down, grasped the hem of my dress, ordered me to raise my arms and, in one movement, peeled off my dress. I stood there in my underwear and shoes, waiting to see what would happen next. There had been no initial conversation, as is normally the case between spanker and spankee, especially if they haven't met before, as in this instance. He just took me by the arm, sat me down on the sofa, sat next to me, his hand went down the front of my knickers and before I knew it, I'd had an orgasm. This very much surprised me. I usually have to feel very at ease with a guy before I can climax. Then he made me bend over the bed, with arms and hands on the bed, knees on the floor, and started using the riding crop, gently at first, over my knickers. He took down my knickers and the strokes got harder.

Throughout the session with him, he would suddenly bend me over furniture and thrash me with the crop. He never used any other implement, even his hand. A crop is malleable, so although it stung, it didn't bruise. Then bizarrely, he would suddenly stand me up and hold me in the slow dance position while staring into my eyes, which I found very disconcerting. I tried to avert my stare from his eyes.

At one point, he ordered me into bed, where he tried for about thirty minutes unsuccessfully to give me another orgasm with his hand. I tried very hard not to touch him at all. I knew I wasn't obliged to get into bed. I had made it clear from my spankee web page that I would not perform any sexual acts. I submitted to the hand massage in the bed as a favour, although I also thought I might enjoy it, and he emphasised that he didn't expect anything from me in return. While I lay naked in the bed, he kept taking the sheets back, ordering me onto all fours and whipping me four or five times fairly hard with the crop.

At the end of the session, he asked if I'd like to go downstairs to the hotel bar and have a drink. I agreed out of politeness and as we headed down, I noticed he left his coat and laptop in the room. Over drinks, he said he'd never thrashed anyone as hard as he had done with me. I was so proud! He also told me he was surprised I had got into the bed and had let him go that far with his hands. Most spankees said no at that point, he stated. He turned out to be a retired gynaecologist (or so he told me).

I finished my drink before him and got up to go but realised I had left my phone in the room.

'Here's the key. I will be up shortly,' he said, without any hesitation.

'That's very trusting of you,' I told him.

'No problem. I trust you.' He smiled up at me. He was right to trust me, as I had no intention of stealing his laptop, but I felt it was quite a risk he was taking. But I noticed that that seemed a common thread within the spanking community. Treat others as you would like to be treated.

*****

Some spankers went to great lengths to create a realistic and sexy scenario for a spanking session. One 60-year-old spanker asked me to make out a 'sin list' – a list of things I had done in the previous few weeks that I considered punishable. As soon as I started this list I realised there were quite a few. They included uncharitable thoughts about people, such as hoping a friend of the family wouldn't ring to arrange a visit, being pleased someone at work I didn't like had put on even more weight, and being too lazy to vacuum my house for a friend's visit.

He met me at Nottingham station, put my arm through his and walked me to a nearby hotel. Once inside the room, he asked to see my list of sins. He sat me down on a chair opposite him and proceeded to berate me for each crime in turn from the list, describing the number of strokes I was going to receive, the severity of each stroke, and with which implement. I was to be spanked, strapped, belted and caned. For some of the punishment, I would be naked and tied with rope to a chair. Over the course of three hours, during which he produced a delicious lunch and chatted to me amicably, I took 128 strokes of the cane and 126 strokes of the belt. I know because he insisted with each one that I count them and say 'Thank you, Master'. If I ever addressed him, I had to use the term 'Master' at the end of every sentence, otherwise he would add two more strokes of the cane to the next punishment. He let me off the first omission of 'Master', but on the second and third omission, I received two more strokes of the cane.

At one point, I was completely naked and tied with rope by my ankles to the legs of a chair. Another rope went from my ankles up around my elbows, down round my crotch, round my back and around leather handcuffs on my wrists. I felt very vulnerable and decided not to agree to this degree of restraint again with any other spanker, but I had agreed beforehand to be tied up, and didn't want to renege. Part of me wanted to see just how far he would go.

After giving me twelve strokes while I was tied to, and slightly bent over, the chair, he undid the rope round my ankles and ordered me onto the bed, still trussed up like a mummy. I could hardly walk. I was worried I would hurt my breasts when getting onto the bed as my elbows were still tied back, so he had to help me by lowering me gently onto my front. My bottom stuck up at a conveniently spankable angle from the bed. I received another caning and belting while he continued to berate me for the worst sins on the list. He seemed to be a very experienced spanker and carried out the strokes in such a way that I was hardly bruised the next day. He gave me frequent hand rubs and caresses throughout the day between sets of strokes and then rubbed moisturising cream over my sore bottom every now and then.

The next day I received an email saying how well I'd taken the punishment, inviting me to spend a week with him on his boat on a Greek island and hinting that he'd like me to be his girlfriend. Unfortunately, I had to decline this delightful invitation as he held no attraction for me. If only. He didn't take kindly to the rejection. Another client bites the dust.

*****

Another spanker contacted me with a polite, introductory email so I replied and we agreed to chat on the phone. He sounded fun and emphasised that he only wanted to use his hand and a slipper. Not the cane, I was pleased to hear. We arranged to have our first session and then I received this unexpected email:

'*Dear Lily-Rose,*
Your husband will have made you aware that you would be contacted by me.
Your current behaviour is quite unacceptable and your husband has made you aware of his displeasure, but lacks the fortitude to take remedial action to curb your behaviour.
You will attend my offices on September the 25th at no later than 19.00.
You will bring with you, your husband's slipper and a plimsoll.
You will be dressed and act in an appropriate lady-like manner, I can assure you now that you will be receiving a prolonged hand spanking and a severe slippering for your slovenliness and inappropriate behaviour.
I would be grateful if you could confirm your acceptance of this punishment and I will report your cooperation to your husband.
Kind regards'

I found the idea of being sent by one man to be spanked by another somehow erotic. We met up and the session was cordial and fun – but gone was the dominant, confident guy in the second email. I was placed over his knee, fully dressed, and hand spanked for five minutes, then the slipper was used on me over my skirt. He suddenly admitted that he was a fairly new spanker. Only once did he take my knickers down, having asked very politely beforehand, and gave me four or five shy taps with the slipper, only to quickly bring the knickers up again, as if he thought that was overstepping the mark.

One thing he kept doing that was unusual was to take hold of me by the ear in order to change my position from, say, over a chair to over the bed. He only released his grip when I'd reached the new position. I squealed a few times, but he said I deserved it and I should learn to take it. All part of the role-play I realised, but slightly outside of the boundaries I felt, although I let him carry on. I had to sometimes walk a fine path between pain and letting the spanker carry out his fantasies to give him his money's worth, and allow the scenarios to play out seamlessly.

When the session was over, he invited me for a plate of chips and a drink in the nearby pub. He was much younger than me, so a date was not on the horizon. Out in the car park, he said he might contact me again in about six months' time, which I took to mean I wouldn't hear from him again. This turned out to be the case.

I used to forget that a spanking session can be quite an ordeal for new spankers as well as spankees. It can be awkward engineering the positions a spankee will be placed in, especially if you are not a particularly dominant person in normal society. Hence, I think, the use of the ear grip, which prevented him having to say, 'Er – could you put yourself over the chair now please.'

*****

I also heard stories of girls being spanked for 'real' discipline. A man who liked spanking for fun one day discovered that his ex-girlfriend had become so jealous of his current girlfriend that she had threatened her with a knife. He thought of going to the police, but decided that a caning would actually be kinder. She would learn her lesson and not be tarnished with a criminal record.

He went round to her house and stood on her doorstep, holding a cane very visibly. Partly because she wanted him back and partly because she didn't want the neighbours to see, she allowed him into the house. He wasted no time in spanking her over his knee very hard for about three minutes, berating her behaviour, while she howled and screamed. He then hauled her over the back of the sofa, and, holding her down with his hand in the small of her back, caned her twelve times – six over the knickers, and six with knickers down. They didn't have any trouble from her again.

*****

Another man had been punished by a female friend of the family when he was a teenager. He had done no more than try and get her teenage daughter into bed. The mother found out and had put him across her knee, using a hairbrush on his bare bottom. He never forgot the humiliation of it, fearing his testicles and anus were on display. Years later, as a strapping guy of over six feet, he got his own back by spanking her over his knee with a hairbrush on two separate occasions. She thrashed around and yelled, but the punishment carried on until he'd had his revenge.

*****

The line between abuse or discipline and erotic fun must be fairly thin in many instances. I had heard of 'maintenance spankings', where a husband regularly spanks his wife to keep her on her toes. He might also give her an extra hard spanking before they go out for the night, saying that if she stepped out of line during the evening, she could expect another spanking of equal severity on her return. But I also heard of a cruel case where a man tied his wife up over a bench in their garden shed for four hours while he went out. When he came back, he thrashed her with a cane until she bled and then had sex with her while she was still tied up over the bench.

Chapter 15

Taking Stock

I had been a spankee for about a year now and had made about £3000. It was useful money, and stopped me having to dig into my bank account for monthly bills, but at this rate, it was going to take a long time to pay off the £20,000 debt my husband had kindly left me.

I could only normally take one spanking a week, at £100 an hour, the normal fee for a whole spanking session, even if it lengthened to two hours due to chatting or having a glass of wine. This was partly because I was still in full-time employment but also because I bruised very easily and often bore the remnants of a spanking for several days afterwards, especially if I'd been caned. Spankers prefer to have a blank canvas to work on. Partly for humane reasons, they don't like to spank or cane a bruised bottom, but also they don't like to see the handiwork of another man on their spankee. They know only too well that spankees are spanked by other men, but for the sake of the make-believe scene they have conjured up for a session, it's nicer to have an unblemished bottom before them, belonging to a naughty girl who needs a good spanking from them alone.

I had originally entered the CP world to get rid of the debt, but spanking had now become so much more to me. It had become part of my life. I was becoming good friends with some of the spankers, and I wasn't sure I wanted to give any of it up. It's just a convenient symbiosis. Spankers enjoy spanking, and spankees enjoy being spanked. Some spankees enjoy it so much they can orgasm from a spanking. Although I undoubtedly found it all sexy, I didn't even come close to climaxing, and, in fact, it never entered my head that CP punishment alone could give me an orgasm. If it was a caning, I was too busy dealing with the current pain and fearful of what pain was about to be unleashed.

Time and again, spankers appreciated the fact that I was very turned on by a session. Most of them didn't enjoy it if they could see that the spankee had just turned up, bent over, taken the spanking, then the money, and left, with hardly any social or sexy interaction. Some young spankees were having three sessions a day, so I could understand that after a while it became more like a job to them.

A spanker told me about a session he'd had which he didn't really enjoy as the spankee was very unexcited by the whole event. She was an attractive, slim, twenty-seven-year-old girl, who lived with her sixty-seven-year-old master, who was also her boyfriend. After the initial social chit-chat, the spanker finally got to spank her but was watched the entire time by the master, who sat opposite them.

After a while, the master suggested the client feel between her legs. She was as dry as a bone, which made the spanker begin to feel rather emasculated. In order to try and get a sexual reaction out of her, the master ordered her to strip naked in front of them, stand facing them, hands on head and spread her legs, whereupon he started to spank her crotch from the front. Not a drip appeared between her legs.

The spanker was then allowed to adjourn upstairs with her alone to have oral and vaginal sex. He likened the whole episode to 'fucking a robot' since they had to use a lubricant to achieve penetration. He had found it hard to keep an erection. He was relieved when it was all over and he could leave a session that hadn't given him anything but some dented male pride. Perhaps I should have lent her some of my HRT.

A few spankers asked if they could sexually penetrate me while I lay over their knee or a table or back of a sofa. I refused (politely) and they didn't press the matter, not expecting me to agree anyway.

It wasn't that I hadn't contemplated it with one or two of them, especially as I was hugely turned on by all the goings-on. But I didn't want to get the reputation of having sex for money, as surely that would make me a prostitute. I outlined my reason for my refusal to one of the spankers, and he immediately said, 'No, you're being given money to be spanked. We could just have sex as two consenting adults as a bonus.'

I heard this argument several times. Spankers, without a doubt, don't view spankees as prostitutes at all, even if playful fingering is part of the spanking session. Spankers and spankees alike are all contributing to a fun, erotic scenario. The sex would be just a natural extension of the interaction for both parties to enjoy equally – or so their argument goes.

Chapter 16

The Studio

I had heard from spankers that there were studios that spankees or spankers could hire for £20 an hour. Blue told me he had spanked a girl in one of them but had been annoyed by other spankees interrupting his session by entering the room to fetch spanking implements they had left there. He said it ruined the atmosphere of punishment he had created and made him feel he was on a conveyor belt of customers. So when a spanker suggested meeting at a studio, I was a bit dubious, but decided to try it for the experience.

I met him for a quick cup of coffee a few days before the studio outing so we could check each other out. He was about sixty, seemed friendly and straightforward, and really just wanted a bottom to spank.

During the days between the coffee and the spanking session, I received many texts from him, describing how excited he was at the thought of caning me naked over one of the whipping benches. He would ask at the end of each text if I was also excited at the prospect of the session with him. I replied to the first few that I was, but then, rather unprofessionally, left many of them unanswered.

On the appointed day, we met in a petrol station, and I followed his car down some narrow Birmingham back streets until we turned into a small courtyard surrounded by tumbledown ruins. Two men, wearing brown raincoats and aged about fifty, were waiting outside the door of one of the ruins, one of them smoking. If this had been a gangland movie, it would have been a cliché. I felt I had stooped quite low, even for me, to have to use such a desolate place.

My spanker paid the smoking guy £20 and was handed a key. It was the first time I felt like a prostitute and her pimp. We went in through a dilapidated door and up some rickety stairs, which looked as if we would fall through them at any moment. After reaching the first floor, we went through another creaky door to the studio. I was pleasantly surprised. A large room was loosely divided into three smaller open-plan rooms. Each was expertly furnished to look like a headmaster's or manager's office. Each had a whipping bench, I noticed straight away, with some trepidation. There were chaises longues, armchairs, sofas, chairs, desks and tables to bend over. On one of the tables was an impressive array of canes, whips, straps, belts, paddles and riding crops for anyone to use.

We had the rooms to ourselves, so we knew we could role-play without interruption. I was becoming better at acting out my role as naughty schoolgirl, errant secretary or recalcitrant apple-stealer without ruining it by laughing through nerves or self-consciousness. This time I had been caught pilfering the petty cash and a good spanking was in order, followed by a caning over each of the three whipping benches in turn. The spanker said he sometimes tied girls to the whipping benches, but, as it was my first time, he didn't want to scare me.

His role-play lasted about twenty seconds, and mine lasted no more than five seconds, during which I managed to mumble that I certainly hadn't stolen anything, whereupon he asked me to choose which cane I would like him to use. I chose the lightest and thinnest I could see, but he proceeded to use all of them anyway. And he didn't hold back when using the straps, paddles or canes, as my bottom bore witness to over the next few days. But I was surprised how much more fun it was having a realistic set-up as a backdrop, and thought I might well hire it out another time.

A week after this session, I was sitting with a date watching a play at the Royal Shakespeare Theatre in Stratford. I wore a nice little white dress and a lacy shawl. From being thrashed over whipping benches with my legs apart, to looking demure and cultured, knees firmly together, watching Shakespeare – such was my double life. I have to say I was enjoying not only the secrecy but the life itself.

Chapter 17

Dating and Spanking

I had been trying out the dating sites for about three years and had managed to meet forty-four men without finding any that were suitable. Thirty-eight liked me more than I liked them. I was ambivalent towards the six who decided I wasn't the one for them after one date anyway, but I would definitely have gone on a second date to make sure.

I went out with a few for more than one date, but there always seemed to be one major flaw that was just too awful to make them eligible as a life partner. For several, it was patience. Or the lack thereof. Some were too overweight. Others had long nasal hair or bad breath, BO or groin odour.

One particularly nice guy, who seemed otherwise perfect from the two dates I had with him, turned out not to have enough money to his name to even pay for his half of a meal. Been there. Not doing that one again. I would end up paying for everything, which would eventually cause resentment.

For many, it was talking too much and not listening enough. Not enough *interested* listening. Yes, they might have been nervous, but I was also nervous, and I ended up doing most of the listening. Strange that so many people (men and women) think other people want to sit and listen to them spouting on, without showing any interest in the other person's life. The date would end and they would say they had had a nice time – and not found out almost anything about me, their date. Their potential future partner. I ended up feeling boring, as well as bored and uninspired, and would momentarily lose the will to live.

I worked on the premise that if a conversation didn't flow relatively smoothly from the beginning, a partnership was probably not going to work either. This may have been too harsh, but after many dates, I had become weary of the effort it took to initiate some kind of spark. I looked for common ground, especially shared interests and hobbies on which to build a conversation, and possibly a relationship. I also looked for a common sense of humour.

I dared to wonder and, in fact, hope that dating and spanking would merge into one perfect man, who would obviously live within ten minutes of my house.

*****

Dating and spanking did take place together on several occasions, but as ever in life, not the way I had envisaged.

I persuaded a good-looking guy on one of the dating sites, who lived about fifteen minutes away from me, to meet for a coffee. For some reason, we didn't have the normal pre-date telephone call, where we would probably both have realised we weren't suited at all. He turned out to be an ex-soldier. We had very different backgrounds, senses of humour and dress sense. It was obvious there was to be no second date, but in our post-date final texting, I decided to mention that I was a spankee. He immediately rang and said he was intrigued. I told him a bit about it, and after a pause, he said:

'What are you wearing?'

'Er – a short black skirt.'

'Well, bend over the nearest table. Put your hand down the front of your …'

Phone sex! I had never seen the point, and the guy clearly had the wrong idea.

'No, sorry. It doesn't work like that.' I brought the conversation to a swift end.

*****

The 38th guy I met through the dating site started off contacting me through the spankee site, not knowing I was also on his dating site. He couldn't have known since my face was not visible on the spankee site, and I used a different name. His opening email was well-written and polite. Here it is below verbatim, with some names and locations changed:

'Hi Lily-Rose,
I saw your page on spankee****** and of course I am interested in the possibility of you you coming to my home for a relaxed spanking.
My home is in the North Cotswolds, north of Santon, so perhaps you might like to consider that from a travelling point of view?
You will find me reasonably well experienced in administering a spanking, which hopefully will set you at ease, as well as providing pleasure for both of us.
I look forward to hearing from you very soon to see what we might arrange.
Best regards,
W'

After the obligatory initial phone call to ensure he was reasonably 'normal', I arranged to go to his house a few days later. I wore a figure-hugging knee-length black sleeveless dress with a white trim on the arms and hem.

As I was parking outside his house, I became aware of a man standing on the pavement overseeing the operation. He was about 5' 8" tall, stocky, with a good head of hair and a full bushy beard. I recognised him straight away. I wound down the car window.

'I recognise you from the Match.com website,' I said brazenly. He looked at me in surprised silence, trying to see if there was reciprocal recognition.

'Oh. You're right in that I am on that site. But sorry – I don't recognise you.'

'That's OK,' I laughed. 'There are hundreds of people on dating sites. You can't know everyone.'

It broke the ice and, once inside, we chatted away easily about dating and spanking while having a cup of tea in his comfortable lounge. I sat at one end of a very deep, plush, lilac-grey sofa and he on a hard chair about six feet away. It was so cordial that I wondered if he might find it difficult to broach the subject of spanking me.

He introduced himself as William, but I knew that often the first name I was told would turn out to be a cover name used only within the CP scene. I could hardly complain. I was there as Lily-Rose.

He had been spanking for a few years and only ever did it in his house, never a Travelodge or hotel. He didn't do it very often, partly because he couldn't afford it, but also because the girl had to be just right. Small, slim, and not too young. I guess I fitted the bill.

He said he had wanted to spank for a long time, but when he had broached the subject with his then-wife after they had just got married, she had just chuckled and said, 'Don't be silly.' So he had managed to spank only a few girls occasionally when his wife was away on business.

He actually spanked his wife once in anger, he told me. She had borrowed his car and totalled it. So he'd had to buy another one, which she also totalled.

'I'm going to spank you,' he warned her.

'You are NOT!' she shouted back, defiantly.

But he caught her and hauled her over his knee in their lounge and spanked her hard for a few minutes. She yelled out, but he carried on. She didn't speak to him for a week afterwards.

It was unusual to hear of a spanking carried out in anger within a loving relationship, although perhaps since they were now divorced the relationship had reached a not-so-loving stage. Usually, a spanking is the fun, consensual prelude to sexual activity. If a couple is in the middle of a heated argument, the last thing on their minds would be a spanking. One or the other of them would be too annoyed to participate. A fact which aptly demonstrates the degree to which the 'punishment' side of CP spankings is normally purely a contrived excuse for eroticism.

Although it was interesting that any pretence of punishment should often have to exist at all. Why not just get straight down to the spanking? Perhaps it affords both participants the build-up and anticipation that is needed to enhance sexual excitement and stimulation.

As for dating, William confided that his choice of women had been somewhat detrimental to his mental health. His last girlfriend demanded oral sex every morning before they went to work, venting her fury if he didn't manage to give her an orgasm every time. She also had such an insecure, jealous nature that if they were standing together in the pay queue of a department store, and she noticed a pretty girl behind one of the payment points, she would stand in front of William as they made their way up the queue, to stop him seeing her. I didn't ask what happened if the same girl happened to be the one that eventually took their payment.

There was a pause in William's and my conversation. We had both finished our tea. Without saying anything, William got up awkwardly and sat down in the middle of the sofa next to me. He patted his thigh nearest to me, still without a word. I stood up and put myself over his knee. There was apparently not going to be any fanciful scenario of punishment. He started spanking me over my dress, very gently. I waited for my dress to be raised but it didn't happen. It was possibly embarrassment that made him hesitate. The spanking became slightly harder but I couldn't class it as pain. Not with my thickened skin and over two layers of clothing.

After about three minutes, he stopped and said rather gingerly, 'Er – I'd like to go into the bedroom with you and feel you under your clothes while you bend over the bed.' 'Yes, sure,' I said immediately. He was paying, after all. As long as he didn't expect anything approaching sex from me.

I bent over the bed and remembered to arch my back so that my bottom was presented well. I felt my dress being lifted from behind and my knickers taken down to my knees. His hand slipped between my legs and I felt him caressing me.

Mid-caress, he suddenly said, 'Would you like to go for a coffee sometime? I mean, nothing to do with spanking.'

This took me by surprise, but as I did find him quite attractive, I agreed. It would have been awkward to refuse since he knew that I was single from our initial chit-chat about dating. But I was flattered and admired his courage in making such a brave offer. I thought it was time to merge dating and spanking. It could surely only enhance our sex life, if indeed it came to that.

Our first date was a coffee in a grubby little cafe in a nearby town. Very cordial. Nothing stressful. We chatted very easily about spanking mostly and past relationships. I noticed, though, that even during this first date, he started talking about the future with me. This was flattering but way too soon for me. It was winter and he mentioned where he would like to go for a summer holiday with me. I didn't say anything but was just aware that this might be a warning of things to come.

We didn't go back to his house after that first date. Instead, we made arrangements to meet up again the following weekend. Rather ironic that there was no mention of sex even though he had already had his hand between my legs, and my knickers round my knees.

The next weekend we went to watch the Severn Bore roll magnificently up through the Severn Valley, with several surfers in black wetsuits riding the wave as it passed us. It was cold, wet and windy, and as we stood on the side of the river, I started to shiver so snuggled into his coat for warmth. He seemed happy to be there, enjoying our date, his arm around me. We had a meal in a pub, and again he started talking about the future, asking me the sort of house I might like to live in with him. I dodged the question by just laughing and saying, 'Ooh, I don't know.'

During the following week, I received many emails from him, stressing how much he liked me and broaching the subject of sleeping together without a hint of spanking first. Quite interesting the way he separated the two. He either wanted to go out with me, or spank me. Or perhaps he just wanted to show me respect at the beginning of the relationship.

But unfortunately, I didn't feel the same way and had to let him down as gently as I could. Many sad emails from him followed, saying how much he had enjoyed helping me to keep warm as I shivered in his arms on the edge of the Severn. After yet another email from me rejecting his advances, he made one final attempt to see me again.

'OK,' he said, determined to try anything, 'Let's just meet up to spank, pure and simple.'

I rejected this suggestion since it would never have worked, and he probably knew it. He had too many feelings for me and would have been constantly hoping that I might change my mind. I wished I had never agreed to go out with him, since I had now lost a client.

*****

A Scottish surgeon, who had worked in A & E for many years, contacted me. Our initial email conversation suggested that he would probably be a considerate spanker, and have my wellbeing in mind. I include the first few emails here below verbatim, apart from changing names and locations:

'i have read your advertisement and am interested in an appointment. i am 58 yr old man, single ,5'11" 14-15 stone. i have always enjoyed spanking
  i live in Tenningworth so perhaps hotel/lodge would be best if possible i would be interested in appt on 13th or 27th April
  i hope you are interested.
  please ask me anything you might want to know.

Daniel xx'

This was early on in my spanking career, so I had to be careful that his expectations weren't more than I could supply. I wasn't even charging the normal £100 an hour, as I considered myself such a novice:

'Hi Daniel

Thanks for your message.

A hotel/lodge would be fine. My rates are £70 for the first hour and £50 per hour pro-rata after that. I don't switch and as yet have only had 1 session with the hand and slipper. At some point I will try the belt and strap but I need to ease myself gently towards that I think.

Definitely not the cane at the moment – sorry!

Hope this is something you're interested in.

Kind regards,

- Lily-Rose'

'I am interested.

I suggest 13th April.

I can book room at travelodge Birmingham airport hotel.

I would like to book 2 hours with you.

Maybe 3pm to 5pm or something like that.

Are you interested?

Daniel'

'Hi Daniel,

Sorry - there are other things I should have explained.

You would have to pay for the room as well.

Last time I only managed 1 hour, as my bottom was turning blue and purple from the slipper. I might only manage an hour this time. I've since bought a more girlie slipper so it should only sting rather than bruise.

What would you like me to turn up in? Don't worry – I will disguise it if it looks too tarty. lol.

Meant to say - I can only make the 27th I'm afraid. I already have an appointment on the 16th so I'm worried that if I see you on the 13th my bottom might not have recovered by the 16th.

Could you tell me a bit about yourself. Age, cp experience, cp preferences.

Thanks,

Regards,

– Lily-Rose'

'I understood that I would pay for the room.
27th April is fine then.
Only one hour is ok.
I have always been interested in cp but only recently started actually doing it
Most of my pleasure comes from giving you pleasure.
I don't want to really hurt you.
You would have a safe word (eg RED). If u say that word I will immediately stop.
I like to mix regular rubbing with spanking to avoid bruising.
I think u will leave with a nice warm pink bottom.
Would it be possible for u to wear stockings, suspenders and frilly panties?
I am 58 a very recently retired doctor looking to enjoy a 'hobby' of mine.
Daniel.'

'OK – thanks for your flexibility.
Stockings and suspenders are absolutely fine. Would the knickers on the website be any good for you? I have a short-ish black skirt. Any top you'd like?
That's fine for the 27th April then. What time would suit you? I can make most times throughout that day, and would try and make 2 hours if my bottom can agree.
I do allow touching if you would like, but don't give sexual favours. Just to check that you're aware that I'm not into switching.
Lily-Rose.'

'Yes the panties on the photo are fine. Top doesn't matter. Regarding time 3pm or 4pm would suit me best. I'm not interested in switching myself.
Don't worry about 1 or 2 hours. Once u stop enjoying yourself I'm not interested in continuing. I understand no sexual favours but like to tease u a little with gentle touching.
Daniel.'

We duly met up in the Birmingham Travelodge. We chatted for about twenty minutes over tea, biscuits and crisps, which he scattered liberally over the bed. I lay on the bed in my jeans, up against the pillows, happily eating the snacks he'd provided. He sat on one of the chairs on the other side of the room. He was a charming man, intelligent and interesting. He had taken early retirement from working in A & E because it was too stressful. He said life was too short for so much stress, and now he was pursuing other, more calming interests.

'Right,' he finally said, looking very relaxed and pleased with the current situation, 'I'd like to start now. Please go into the bathroom and get dressed.'

It always took me longer than I wanted to change into my spankee clothes if there were suspenders involved. I hadn't worn suspenders since I was sixteen and the clasp kept slipping from my fingers, especially if I was nervous. I would be aware that there was an expectant client waiting for me on the other side of the bathroom door. On this occasion, the clasp kept pinging off.

Spankers would often like me to knock on the inside of the bathroom door and wait for them to give me permission to enter the bedroom again. This would unconsciously set a different atmosphere between us than the cordial, social one that had been taking place minutes before, when we would be doing things like, as in this case, munching crisps and biscuits.

I was finally ready to knock on the inside of the bathroom door. 'Come in,' he called seriously. 'Please have a seat on the bed. I would like to begin by setting the scene for us. You don't have to say anything.'

I liked the sound of that. It was early days and I still dreaded having to act out a role. He got up and sat on the other side of the bed from where I was lying and started his story, which he had obviously rehearsed:

'A long time ago, there was a village in a strange land far away. There had been a spate of thefts from local traders in recent weeks but the culprit hadn't been caught, although they somehow knew it was a young girl. The king of the village decided that every unmarried girl in the village would be spanked or caned until the thief came forward. He hoped the thieving girl would feel guilty for causing such punishment to all the village girls.'

Rather ingenious, I thought.

Daniel then looked at me and said, 'Come and get your spanking.' So I put myself over his knee and lay with my top half across the bed. He was a considerate spanker, as I thought he would be, and gave me frequent rubs. He used his hand over my skirt for a few minutes, then my black skirt came up to reveal the beige, lacy knickers and black suspenders and stockings he'd asked for. He spanked one buttock about three times and then the other, becoming progressively harder with each change of buttock. It was stinging, since I was still quite new to the scene, and my bottom had not yet developed the thick, rougher layer it was to form a few months later.

After a good fifteen minutes of this on-and-off hand-spanking, he said, 'I would really like to use the cane on you. Would you like to try it? I promise I will stop as soon as you tell me to.'

Even though I had told him I couldn't take the cane, I did want to try it again. I had tried it once before with another spanker and had found the pain very difficult to take.

'OK. I will try a few and see what I can take.' Caning seemed to be the pinnacle of many spankers' dreams, the holy grail of CP.

'Excellent. Put yourself over the back of that chair.'

I bent right over the chair with the typical Travelodge blue felt covering, with my hands on the seat. I felt him approach me. He wasted no time in pulling my knickers down to my knees. Then I felt a light cane being placed gently on my already smarting bottom, and I remember staring at the blue of the chair as I waited, waited, waited. I heard the swish of the cane through the air as it was brought down with a thwack on both buttocks at once. I gasped at the stinging pain. But the pain dissipated immediately, which surprised me, so I felt I could take a few more. As I didn't complain, he raised the cane again, and down it came again with the same force. Each time I heard the swish through the air before feeling the cutting stroke. I gasped each time. It was a sound that I had never heard myself use before, and ever after that during my life as a spankee, this sound emanated from me, without my even wanting it to.

He made me count the strokes. When I reached five, he rubbed my bottom. His hand slipped between my buttocks and he started caressing me. I didn't say anything so he continued in silence. Then he took up the cane again and gave me five more strokes of the same intensity. He definitely knew what he was doing, as the pain vanished straight away and each new stroke didn't seem to hurt any more than the previous one, as if there had been no bruising.

'Have you had enough?' he enquired nicely. 'You've done very well, I must say. And you have a gorgeous bottom.'

'Yes, I think I have had enough. I'm surprised I could take that many strokes. You must have a good touch.'

I dressed and he handed me an envelope, which had been sitting on the table throughout the session. I still found being paid slightly embarrassing, especially if our interaction had been friendly and cordial. It did make me feel a bit like a prostitute, but I wasn't about to offer free sessions since I needed the money. I shouldn't have felt guilty for accepting money for my service, but at this stage, it was really soooo so alien to anything I had done before. It took me months to get used to the idea that I was actually allowing strange men to pay me to take down my knickers, spank me and feel me in places only boyfriends had previously dared to venture.

He commented that he thought it unfair that men always have to pay for spankings. I did agree with him in fact. I justified this to myself because men know this from the outset, and it is their choice. It is also we women who are taking the pain – and it can be very painful, much more than is just sexually titillating. We are also taking considerable risk when we enter a room with an unknown man.

We parted on good terms, and he suggested meeting up again in a couple of weeks to have a similar session, especially now that he knew I could take the cane so well. I didn't relish the cane and but

I knew it would make me much more attractive to many spankers.

Before the second session, he suggested going for lunch in the nearby diner. During lunch, he asked me if I'd like to go to a show with him, all expenses paid. I wondered if this was a date or whether I was subtly turning into an escort for him, but it didn't really matter. I enjoyed his company so I accepted his invitation.

The evening of the show, unfortunately, proved that we didn't have much in common besides spanking. We found we couldn't find much to talk about and didn't have the same sense of humour. I was worried that if I didn't accept the next date, I would lose him as a client, but he seemed to sense that there was no spark and didn't suggest any more outings.

We did, however, arrange several more spanking and caning sessions. The canings became harder, but I found that if I concentrated on the pattern of the chairs I was bending over and tried to compartmentalise each stroke as being a fleeting mini-second of pain, I could take ten or twenty strokes at a time, while continuing to exhale some weird breathy sound that came from I don't know where.

The punishment scenarios were all very similar, but with a slight change to the reason why all the young girls in the village would conveniently need a good thrashing.

*****

A delightful guy contacted me one day, saying he loved putting a naughty lady over his knee when he was standing up and had one leg up on the bed for the lady to bend over. He was a forty-year-old brickie and liked petite girls. He sounded nice by email and by phone so we met up in a hotel room one afternoon.

He was a big, muscly guy. About 6' 2", he was built like a wrestler or rugby player. His neck must have been wider than my thigh. All he wanted to do was spank me completely naked over his knee while he stood on one leg and bent the other leg up on the bed for me to bend over. I wasn't quite sure how I was going to get up over his knee, but by using the bed as a springboard and with him giving me a hand up, I ended up rather precariously dangling over his bent leg. He started spanking me gently and then asked me to spread my legs. He caressed my lips and then alternated between a gentle spanking and the caress for ten minutes or more. He explained that this was the only position he liked. He could see the girl's lips, and play with them, as well as spank easily.

He turned out to be a gentle giant, a complete softie. He was such an open, friendly guy that I liked him straight away and felt immediately at home with him. He chatted away during the spanking, saying he couldn't find a girlfriend who liked spanking. He had felt the need to spank since puberty but hadn't dared to broach the subject with girlfriends for fear that they would think him weird.

He suddenly stopped, lifted me off his leg as if I was rag doll, lay down on the bed and carried on chatting. Then he suddenly said, 'I'm just going to go for it. Would you like to go on a date?'

My heart sank. I was fifty-eight, he was forty. He was a brickie, I was a middle-class university graduate. I liked playing tennis. He liked going to the pub with his mates and drinking. It would never work, but he was so sweet that I didn't want to reject him out of hand.

'Oh that would have been nice, in fact, but I'm already going out with someone,' I lied.

'Ah OK. That's a shame. We could have had fun together.' He seemed a little crestfallen, but I hoped that he would still want to see me as a client.

The session ended and we left the hotel together. As we parted ways, he couldn't look me in the eyes, and just said, 'OK bye.'

I never heard from him again. Another one bites the dust. I was determined then to try and tell clients before I met them that I already had a partner, to stop them having to have the indignity of a rejection.

*****

Chapter 18

Office Work

A guy contacted me one day saying he'd like to use the cane on me in his office. He worked in a business park only about fifteen minutes from my house. He owned the company so we could use the office when all the staff had gone home for the day. He sounded nice, and I liked the idea of a spanking in an office setting, so, after a quick conversation on the phone, I agreed to meet him.

And so it was that I found myself driving through an unfamiliar business park late one summer evening, looking for an unknown man to cane me. I was wearing a short, flowery, billowing, yellow summer dress. White shoes, lacy white knickers. No bra, as requested.

I turned down a small side street and saw a man standing outside one of the units, having a smoke. He didn't look up as I drove towards him even though he must have guessed who I was. Maybe he was nervous. Only when I finally parked in front of him and got out of the car, did he acknowledge me.

'Good evening,' he said, with a smile, 'let me show you around the premises.'

For the next half hour or so, he proceeded to give me a tour of his office and small factory floor, where car parts were made. He told me all about his company, how he started it, what the future plans were, and the problems he was having. I felt like an interviewee, but I also felt honoured that he was bothering to explain all this to me. He could have just led me into one of the side rooms, caned me, and that would have been it for the evening. But

I sensed after a while that he was procrastinating because he didn't know how to broach the subject of spanking, or start a session.

In fact, the more we chatted about all sorts of subjects – anything but spanking – the more I was convinced he was finding it awkward. So as my back was aching from standing all that time because of a parachuting accident I'd had some years earlier, I decided to open the CP conversation myself, something I'd never had to do before with a client. I had always played the good sub and waited for my dom to suggest the CP activity himself.

'Shall we start the spanking then?' I asked gently.

'Er yes, why not?' he replied. I sensed he was relieved that the subject had at least been broached. 'I've prepared a little room for us.'

He led me into an area that was created out of movable plywood panels, right in the middle of an open-plan office. There was no ceiling to this 'room'. I just hoped that no member of staff had decided to stay late. There was no furniture except for one white plastic chair and one plastic canteen table that would seat four people. The 'walls' were completely bare, and the floor was made up from those cheap, brown, tatty tiles that come to bits easily. The bright office strip lighting from the outer open-plan office shone down on us, preventing any semblance of erotic atmosphere. This was, after all, supposed to be an office spanking. Two small, light canes, one bigger than the other, had been placed on the table, alongside an envelope, which I guessed held my £100 cash payment.

To get things going, I walked over to the table and bent over it.

'Would you like me like this?'

'That would be a good start. I will only spank you tonight with my hand. I don't want to put you off by using the cane on you straight away. We could try that another time.'

I was a bit surprised by this revelation. He had specifically asked to cane me in his email, and he had taken the trouble to lay out two canes on the table. He came over and started spanking me gently with his hand over the dress. After a while, he raised my dress and spanked me over my knickers. But I think the office setting and initial business-like interaction had taken away his appetite, and I felt the spanking was half-hearted. After about three minutes he suddenly said, 'I've just realised I didn't show you the second factory. Perhaps we could restart the spanking there. You might as well take your money now.'

He pushed the envelope into my hand without meeting my eyes.

So off we set on another office tour. The second factory was quite dark, but had many pipes and metal containers at rather convenient spankable heights. This was becoming more interesting. But the guy was intent on explaining how and why this factory was used by his company, and as he headed for the exit that led to the road outside, I realised that that was going to be the end of CP activity that night.

'It was great to meet you,' he said, shaking my hand. 'I'll text you in about a week and we can arrange that caning.'

'Yes, OK. That would be great, especially in that second factory setting.'

'Aha. You're on!' And then, to my surprise, he added, 'I think I will buy another cane just for you and create a dedicated spanking shrine just for Lily-Rose and me to play in after work.'

I liked the sound of that. A regular session and income in an unusual setting conveniently close to my home. But despite his polite show of enthusiasm, I thought it highly unlikely that I would hear from him again. After a week I hadn't heard anything. After six weeks, I still hadn't heard from him, so I decided to text him, as I felt he needed a nudge, and I also rather wanted to try being caned across a container on a dark, atmospheric factory floor. A regular income fifteen minutes from my home was also beckoning.

'Hi. Did you want to try another spanking session?'

Back came the immediate reply, 'Yes I do! Am a bit busy with work at the moment so I will have to get back to you.'

I never heard from him again. I think in his head he had a scenario all worked out, but when it came to reality, it was all too embarrassing.

*****

Another guy wanted to use a gym shoe on me over the boardroom table at his work. He wasn't the boss of the company and so we had to go into the office at the weekend. He wanted me to wear a short, white lacy, summer dress and white shoes.

We met in a department store car park, where I transferred from my car to his. He said he didn't want my car in the company car park in case someone came into work unexpectedly and noticed it.

We were about to drive off when he suddenly remembered that he wanted to buy something in the department store. As he got out of the car, he left the keys in the ignition, and before rushing off to the store, looked in through the window at me and said with a smile, 'I hope you're still here when I get back!'

I was amazed that he would trust me with his car and keys, but really, what would I do with an extra car, when mine was still in the same car park, and he had seen my face and had my phone details?

He drove for about twenty minutes through the streets of Birmingham to a side street. He parked behind a small, dilapidated, white building so that the car wasn't visible from the street. We entered through a side door, which gave onto the main reception area, which was littered with printers and photocopiers of all shapes and sizes. I found out that it was a small, not very profitable printing firm. He led me straight through reception to the back of the building, to a surprisingly impressive modern boardroom, with a huge oval wooden table in the middle of the room and about twenty chairs round it. Normally, I would dread sitting at one of these tables at a stressful work meeting, but this time I viewed it with excitement and slight trepidation.

'Have a seat here.' Taking on a sudden air of authority, he indicated a chair at one end of the table. He took a chair directly opposite me at the other end of the enormous table.

'Right,' he said, and then reading from a piece of paper he

retrieved from his pocket, he continued in a grave manner. 'It has come to my notice that your work lately has been very slovenly. You come in late, and you have been making many mistakes. We have discussed what we can do with you and have decided to give you two choices. You can either leave now, or you will submit to corporal punishment, which will consist of you bending over this table, with your knickers down, and my applying several strokes with a gym shoe to your bottom.'

I joined in the scenario. 'My work is not slovenly. I have been doing very well lately, and I haven't been late either.' I found that I could act out this role-play quite convincingly if I played the recalcitrant secretary, employee etc. and just 'lied' about my recent work achievements.

'I'm afraid several managers have seen you arrive late many times over recent weeks so that is a lie, Ms Rose. Furthermore, they checked your work, and I can confirm that there ARE many mistakes, which is not acceptable. What is your choice, Ms Rose? You go or I take the gym shoe to your behind.'

Just occasionally in these role-plays, I was tempted to say that I would just leave, to see the reaction, but that would, of course, defeat the object, so I would never have done that in reality.

'Well I'm certainly not going to resign,' I retorted defiantly.

This conversation continued for at least five minutes. He was savouring every minute, listing more details of my misdemeanours and work failures, which I strenuously denied. It all took place with great seriousness. I always marvelled at the acting prowess of these ordinary people, who I assumed had had no drama training.

I was just wondering if he would ever start the actual spanking when he finally got up from his chair, walked the length of the table until he reached my chair and stared down at me.

'Bend over the table,' he ordered. I obeyed, with both arms stretched out and elbows flat against the smooth table. I immediately felt his hand on my bottom over my dress. 'I shall spank you for a bit before using the shoe.'

He spanked me gently for about five minutes, then stood back, directly behind me.

'Raise your dress, and take your knickers down just past your bottom.'

I did so, aware that he could then see my lips over the edge of the table. 'I'm going to use the gym shoe now.'

I don't know where he got the shoe from, but I certainly knew when he was using it from the first stroke onwards. It was surprisingly painful and felt as if it was bruising me over quite a large area of my buttocks. It wasn't a bendy shoe, so there was no give, hence the pain. The cane was always a very sharp, cutting pain. This gym shoe was a heavy, dull, wide, bruising thud. After about ten strokes, I started to cry out. He stopped and asked me if I was OK, suddenly concerned.

'Well, it's hurting rather more than I thought. But I'll try and take it a bit longer if you could do it a bit more gently.'

This rather ruined the atmosphere of punishment, but he didn't mind at all. 'Of course. I'll tone it down.' He gave me two more strokes but I said I couldn't take any more. He immediately stopped and then said, jovially, 'I can't stand it. You are lying there with your bottom on display. I want to …. you know.'

I looked round at him to check the seriousness of this statement, but saw that he was smiling and half-joking, although I think he would have gone ahead had I agreed.

'Sorry, I don't do sex.'

'No, no. That's fine.' Then he chuckled. 'Well I really enjoyed that. Perhaps next time we can try it outside somewhere.'

I was relieved that he had enjoyed the session, because, in fact, the spanking part of the whole escapade, from the talking-to at the beginning to the last gym shoe stroke, had really only taken up about fifteen minutes. I think now I should have offered him a part refund, but it didn't cross my mind at the time.

We did meet up again, and tried to find a suitable site for spanking in nearby woods or fields, but something was always 'not quite right'. It was too easily seen from the road, or there were cows around, which would be distracting, or there was nowhere to bend over. So we gave up the idea of outside spanking and had several cordial sessions of pure bare-bottom hand-spanking in hotel rooms, after which his calls stopped coming.

I often didn't find out why clients stopped calling. They were under no obligation to tell me. I could only guess at any number of reasons: they had dropped out of the scene; their wife had found out; their wife had decided she liked the idea of being spanked; they had found a younger spankee; they wanted someone who could take the gym shoe; they couldn't afford it any more. I never asked them either, partly because I didn't want a negative reason, partly because I didn't want to put them on the spot, and partly because it was none of my business.

Chapter 19

A Step Too Far

Another guy, who chain-smoked throughout the session, gave me three strokes of the cane bent over a chair in the middle of his lounge. Then he asked me to undo his belt. I immediately said I wasn't going to perform sexual acts and became quite agitated as he was over six feet and a large man. He calmed me down and said he just wanted me to undo his trousers and his shirt, so that I could suck his nipple while he masturbated. Oh God, how revolting. But I needed the money, so I clamped my mouth around his nipple while he felt me from behind to speed up the process. It was all over in a few minutes. I didn't go back to see him, partly because I didn't want to die from lung cancer. He even invited me to go to New York with him, all expenses paid, for a long weekend, and didn't take too kindly to my rejection. Another client lost.

*****

Two other guys masturbated with one hand and spanked me with the other, and proceeded to deposit their load on my bare back. I was surprised each time how warm it was. They were both then at great pains to wipe my back clean afterwards. I wasn't sure how proud of me my mother would have been at this point.

*****

One guy asked to meet me in a Travelodge near to where I lived. I wore my normal short black skirt, black top, black stockings and high-heeled shoes. It was the middle of the day and often there was no receptionist on duty. This time a lady sat behind the glass and looked up as I entered the lobby. I passed quickly through to the stairs, eyes averted. Probably a dead give-away for someone on a shady mission. I knocked on the door, and a very slight, scrawny, balding man in his mid-forties answered. He appeared to have almost no muscle on his skinny arms. I expected a nice, gentle spanking.

He gave me a small smile and then stood aside to let me walk into the room. He was about 5' 8" tall, wore glasses, and I imagined he might be an accountant. There was very little chat. He didn't seem to want to tell me about himself, his CP experiences or preferences as most people did. He seemed to want to get right down to it without any build-up or pretence of punishment.

'I'd like you to take off your skirt, top, bra, and stockings and bend over the bed, where I shall spank you hard. Keep your knickers and shoes on.'

'OK.'

I did as I was told. He watched as I undressed and bent over the bed, with my elbows on the bed, keeping my legs straight and together. He came over to me and stood beside me. I waited for the onslaught. He started spanking me, one buttock and then the other, gently at first, but soon so hard that I felt my whole body jerk forward with each slap. He carried on like this for about five minutes, not saying a word, just spanking and spanking. The skin on my buttocks was now so thick that hand-spankings didn't cause much pain at all. It was only the cane or the occasional belt swinging round on the side of the buttock that I found painful.

He stopped to take a break and when I stood up to rest my back, I saw that he had walked over to the window and was leaning on the sill, staring at me. To my slight consternation, I suddenly noticed that his flies were undone, and the most gigantic erect penis I had ever seen was protruding from the open zip. From his tiny, weedy body. It looked at least ten inches long. He was massaging it gently.

I'd have loved to have fetched a tape measure and measured it but that might have killed the moment somewhat. I pitied the women who had slept, or tried to sleep, with him. How could all that flesh possibly have fitted inside another human being? Perhaps that was why he had to resort to spankees for gratification. Perhaps all his sexual partners had died during intercourse.

'Don't worry,' he said gently, seeing my concerned expression, 'I'm not going to ask you to touch me. I know that's not what you do. I would just like you to go over to the wall and rub your body up and down and stick your bottom out.' He indicated a stand-alone wall about four inches thick, jutting out from the bathroom into the room.

He sat down on one of the chairs, fully dressed, except for his colossal appendage, which he continued to fondle, and watched as I gyrated up and down the wall like a pole dancer, remembering to keep my very red bottom presented. After a while, he told me to bend over the bed again, so that he could feel between my legs and spank me again. He pulled down my knickers to my knees, and with one hand between my legs and the other hand masturbating himself, he tried for many minutes to reach orgasm without success.

He gave up and said we might as well call it a day. We had to return the key to the front desk, and as we walked into the lobby, trying nonchalantly not to look like a prostitute and client, I saw that the same lady was on reception. I caught her eye as I pushed the key through the used-key slot and quickly looked away. If a woman arrives in the afternoon and checks out after two hours, I reckoned it was unlikely to be a business meeting. Perhaps the receptionist saw this type of thing all the time. No doubt she couldn't care less.

I didn't really enjoy being the masturbatory sex object for clients. I was officially there only to be spanked. But I did reluctantly allow this sort of behaviour since it didn't require any effort on my part and didn't hurt. It was difficult to see it coming or predict who was going to turn a spanking session into one of masturbation. In a way,

I could see that it was harmless, but with new clients, I didn't know what it might lead to. I did have a few regular clients who often masturbated after a spanking with me, but I knew they were not dangerous people. Even so, I wished they wouldn't. I found it hard to say no, wanting to please the client so I earned their repeat custom.

I heard my inner voice saying, 'Well, what do you expect, if you present your bare butt to men'. Fair comment, but my website *had* said no sex, my other inner voice wailed. I was supposed to be just a spankee. At least these masturbating men weren't suggesting sex. And ironically, part of me was secretly proud that I was turning them on, as this must mean they liked my body. Vanity won through.

*****

About a year into my spankeeship, the tall guy I had met at Heathrow Airport suggested we had an afternoon in London with a long spanking session included. He offered to pay me £500, as well as all expenses paid. We would have a meal and maybe go to a show. Did this make me an escort? No, because escorts are expected to have sex as well. I had heard of escorts being just that though – companions for lonely, rich men. In fact, I didn't really care what it was called. It made me whatever I chose to be called. But it was a step in a different direction from being just a spankee, since he was paying me for my company as well.

Anyway, the £500 sounded like easy money to me, so I thought I would go ahead and try it. I met him at Waterloo Station (I was five minutes late), and we went straight to the hotel. I was wearing quite a thick, knee-length, black, pleated skirt, which I assumed he would remove, but as soon as we were in the room, he told me to bend over the chair and wait for him there, fully clothed. He fetched a cane and, without the usual gentle warm-up, started caning me fairly hard through the skirt, saying I had been late again. I was yelping at the strokes but was determined to take it as long as I could.

After about twenty strokes, he ordered me to remove my skirt in front of him and bend over his knee, where he spanked me quite hard over my knickers for about five minutes. After the caning had already made me tender, the spanking hurt as well, but I didn't complain. I wanted to try and take it since the money was so good, and I hoped there might be a repeat.

Suddenly he stopped, roughly took down my knickers to my knees and fingered me as usual, but this time he had one finger on my anus. He asked if I minded, and as I knew him well by then, I said I didn't.

I cannot see the attraction for anuses. It doesn't do anything for me to have someone touch or play with mine. I certainly don't want to see, touch or play with someone else's. A friend of mine often had to lick her boyfriend's rectum at the beginning of sex, even though she didn't really want to. I'm afraid I would have refused. Rectums are there to evacuate faeces. I can find no connection with sex.

The session ended and we went for a meal. While waiting for the food to arrive, he said quite matter-of-factly that he'd like anal sex with me, as he had always been fascinated by it but never ventured into it. What did I think about that? I said I would consider it. After the meal, we didn't have time for a show, so we had another spanking session in the hotel room, with no anal contact, and then I caught my train home.

During the journey home, I thought about his offer. In my mind, I had taken a further step towards prostitution and I didn't know if I liked it. But again, what did it matter what it was called, as long as I got paid? Who would know? Why was it different from having sex with a boyfriend, as long as a condom was used? We hadn't discussed payment for anal sex. It wasn't to my taste, but I would have been prepared to consider it with him if he paid. He was a very nice guy, intelligent, clean and considerate.

He had said during the meal that he had previously had normal vaginal sex with another spankee and it had changed their relationship afterwards, so he didn't want to go down that route again. Fine with me. More and more spankers had begun to get to know me well enough to feel comfortable suggesting penetrative vaginal sex as well as the CP activity. None of them had suggested paying extra for this service, and to them it was certainly nothing to do with prostitution. They just found the whole scenario so erotic that sex seemed a logical and fulfilling finale. I understood – but I only would have wanted to do it if I was paid extra for it. Most of the spankers weren't my type, although they were all nice people, and I certainly didn't want to have sex face to face, with kissing expected. In addition, I would have insisted on the use of condoms.

For a few days, I considered this option carefully. I now understood so well why women went down this road, so much so that I found myself defending prostitutes in general to a guy at the tennis club – to his surprise, and even to mine. It was almost as if I felt I was one of them. He was talking about a holiday he'd just had in Spain and described how he wouldn't go down a certain road at night because there were prostitutes standing on the road junctions. I suddenly found myself saying, 'Why wouldn't you walk down that road? They wouldn't have harmed you.'

The guy looked at me but decided not to say anything, which I was rather relieved about since I would have had a hard time explaining my slight outburst.

I decided against any sex with spankers. I didn't mind them touching me if they wanted, but there would be no vaginal or anal sex, with or without condoms, and I would not be touching them in any sexual way if I could possibly avoid it. That was to be kept within the boundaries of a relationship. For one thing, there were STDs and AIDS to consider, and it might just change a spanker's attitude for the worse. He might become overly zealous, get violent if I decided against it on occasions, or even be jealous of other spankers. I didn't need the money that much.

The Heathrow spanker had, in fact, independently decided against pursuing this activity with me.

'It wasn't fair of me to ask,' he said kindly, 'You made it clear on your website that you wouldn't perform sexual favours, so I shouldn't have even brought it up.'

*****

The last spanker I saw lived about an hour away. He was disabled and said he had £300 to pay me, if I would just come to be spanked in his home. I assured him that I would come if he could just pay the normal spanking fee of £100 and the petrol costs and that I certainly wouldn't be taking all that money from him.

I arrived at his house in the middle of the afternoon. An elderly, well-dressed gentleman opened the door, took one look at me, and ushered me into a back bedroom without any chat. He had a stick and was limping heavily because of a calliper on his leg. He followed me into the bedroom, came right up to me, turned me to face the bed and then I felt his hand on the back of my head as he bent me over the bed and immediately lifted my short black skirt. No beating about the bush here.

He started spanking me gently, and then started chatting.

'You know what's involved, don't you? I just want a little play at spanking, and have a little feel, if that's OK. I would never hurt or harm you.'

The knickers came down and he felt between my legs.

'If you don't mind, I've got a table tennis bat that I'd like to use on you, but only very gently. Is that OK?'

'That's fine. I'll tell you if it gets too much.'

He gave me ten or twelve wallops with the bat. It stung but I could take it. I just let him continue until he'd had enough.

'Now I'd like you to go over to the corner over there and stand on that stool, facing the corner. I'm going to lift your skirt, look at you and feel you. Is that OK?'

I said it was. This was obviously a tried and tested format for this rather charming guy.

I had to pull my knickers up to get on the stool, which was quite high. It was also a bit narrow and rickety, and I couldn't spread my legs more than about nine inches. He came over, stood behind me with his face directly opposite my bottom. He pulled down my knickers and I felt his fingers gently exploring my whole vaginal area, while I studied the cracked paint on the wall.

After about five minutes, he invited me to lie on the bed and came and sat next to me. He started to explain that he wanted to try using a metal bar to which he would tie my ankles at each end, which would spread my legs wide while I lay on my back. He said many of the other spankees refused so he would completely understand if I didn't want to. By this time, I decided I could trust him, so I agreed. The bar was about an inch in diameter and about three foot long. He took my knickers off and tied the bar to my ankles with small leather straps. Then he just fondled me while chatting away about his life and the other spankees he saw regularly. He said he had never married and was a bit lonely, so the spankees were now his friends and often the only people he saw all week.

I began to feel slightly uncomfortable about being spread-eagled in front of him. He was beginning to get rather turned on, and I started regretting allowing him to tie me up. Then he looked at me and waggled his tongue at me, asking me if I would like him to use his tongue on me. I immediately said no, and asked if he could untie me, which he did straight away.

As I was dressing, he said, 'Right. Would you like a cup of tea? I have biscuits.'

'Yes, please. That would be very nice.' I liked to get to know my clients. It made for a much more convivial atmosphere if we had got to know each other. They would be more likely to come back for more. I knew he wanted the company as well.

We sat in his lounge, having tea, as if we were just getting to know each other, chatting mostly about spanking. I was fully aware that he'd just had his large fingers all over me, and here we were, making polite conversation. I didn't realise then that he was to be my last ever paying client.

He's rung up several times since then over the years. Unfortunately, soon after this visit, I met a new man on one of the dating sites, so sadly I had to decline his every request. I would have liked to have joined this lonely gentleman's regular spankees and have given him the company he craved from time to time.

Chapter 20

Welsh Rarebit

The 39th guy from the dating site was a definite possibility. Six foot one inches tall, shoulders a mile wide, chest the size of a football pitch, thick black glossy hair and short dark beard, good-looking Welsh Robin and I chatted away for three hours on our first date. We met for lunch at a pub between our two houses. He was very easy to talk to because he listened well, unlike so many of the other guys I'd met for first dates. He also laughed at my jokes, which is nearly always a sign that we had the same sense of humour. I learned that he had been to university, but after the first year, he had become disillusioned with his electrical engineering course and decided to set up his own company, selling and installing garden equipment such as jacuzzis, marquees and sheds, all over the country. He said he just couldn't work for someone else.

He'd had a series of fairly long-term relationships but they had ended for various reasons. One had wanted children while he had not. One wanted to get married, which had never been on his agenda. Another one had been an outrageous flirt, such as snogging another guy in front of him at a party, which in the end had proved too much.

As he talked, I realised he was happy in his own company, which is always attractive in someone, but his online profile had stated that he 'would love to explore all the wonderful places with someone special'. He liked sailing and rugby, and was generally interested in sports. We found that we had more in common than the profiles showed. He loved flying and had obtained his Private Pilot's

Licence. He had been paragliding in the Alps. I had done a week's paragliding course. I had also done quite a bit of skydiving in the past. We both had an interest in the paranormal but disliked religion.

Well, it was all perfect. In my mind. Apart from the little problem of his living in South Wales and my living in the Midlands. At the end of the meal, we decided to call it a day. We walked out of the pub into the sunshine and he suddenly turned around and gave me a quick kiss on the lips. We didn't discuss it, but I felt it was crunch time. Would he ask me for a second date? I could see he was searching for the right words to say.

'Er – well, if you are ever passing my town, or I am passing Chorton Common, perhaps we could meet up again,' he said hesitantly.

I sighed inwardly. Here we go again. He had actually been quite difficult to pin down for the first date. I'd had to take the initiative and suggest times and dates, and had waited days for answers. But we had just been chatting happily for the last three hours and he certainly hadn't had to kiss me on the lips.

'Well, wouldn't you like to arrange to meet up? It's not really going to work if we just say we will meet up if we're passing.'

'OK. Send me a text and we can arrange something,' he said, backing off towards his car. Not the answer I was looking for, but I just said 'OK.'

I didn't hear anything that evening, but the following morning I heard the familiar alert on my phone to a new text. It was Robin.

'It was great finally meeting you. I thoroughly enjoyed the evening.'

No hoped-for follow-up suggestion of meeting up again. Perhaps he was testing the waters.

'Me too.' I texted back. 'It was lovely.'

After an hour I hadn't received another text from him, so I suggested we go flying together. He said he would look into it, but about a week later told me his flying club had closed down but didn't suggest any other idea for a date. So I sent what I thought would be my final text saying I was 'happy to leave it' and to contact me if he wanted to meet up in the summer.

I heard nothing for two days. On the third morning, I woke up and switched my mobile on, as usual, not expecting anything. A familiar alert rang out, and in my sleepy grogginess and the half-light of the bedroom, I thought I saw four words rolling past on the top bar of the mobile, as it displayed a message one quick line at a time. It looked as if it was from Robin, but then I thought I saw the phrases 'character trait' and 'spanking bottoms'.

Ah – Robin must have found out about my spankee site, and he doesn't like it. Oh well. So be it. I had become resigned to 'losing' him by then. Then I realised that Robin couldn't possibly have recognised me on the spankee website because my web page didn't show my face, and I was using a false name.

Intrigued, I opened up 'Unread Messages' and was astonished at what I read.

'Before we have a 2nd date I have to tell you about a character trait of mine. I have always liked spanking bottoms within a relationship. Many people don't like it, but some do. I will understand if you aren't interested, and don't want to take the relationship any further.'

What were the chances that a date I actually liked would turn out to be a fellow spanker? I chuckled to myself. That was one of the reasons he was being so cagey about a second date. It was honest and only sensible to find out at an early stage if I would be on board with this unusual activity. I texted back immediately:

'Guess what! I'm a spankee on an official spankee site! I get spanked by men for money.'

Back came the incredulous reply, *'You like spanking?'* I was just about to text back 'No', savouring his disappointment, with the intention of texting again, *'I like BEING spanked'* when he rang.

'Well, well,' he laughed down the phone, 'who'd have thought. That must be a chance in a million.'

Everything had changed in a second. We had a huge interest in common. Spankers and spankees feel quite a strong connection with each other in our clandestine, sexy, erotic world, a world we know is often misunderstood by many people. We knew what this could mean. Our sex life could be really erotic and could continue to be enhanced by spanking scenarios instead of becoming staid like most couples' sex lives.

We chatted and laughed and giggled over the phone for over an hour. He had always had an interest, but only did it within relationships. He wasn't interested in being spanked himself. Perfect for me. At one point in the conversation, he even said, 'If we lived together, I would probably spank you every day. And if we went to a party and you spoke out of turn, you would feel a hand on your shoulder and receive a look from me, and you would know what would be in store for you back at home.'

I had to admit that it sounded very sexy (if a little controlling), even if we were jumping the gun slightly. I said that if we were to have a relationship, I would curb my activities with spankers by not permitting any sexual touching by them, but he said he wouldn't mind, as long as I didn't have sex with them. I assured him I wouldn't, but his reply was an ominous 'Hmmm'. He'd had the experience of unfaithful girlfriends before, and wasn't going to be convinced easily.

Then he told me he sometimes used the cane for discipline within a relationship, but only very rarely. Good grief! I didn't want that. That certainly wasn't my idea of a loving, equal relationship. I wanted to be able to giggle with my partner, not be afraid of him. Using the cane smacked of domestic abuse.

What had the poor girls done to deserve such punishment? I had to ask. He said he had carried out a caning on one girlfriend who he'd discovered had had sex with an ex-boyfriend while he was away. She apparently had second thoughts about a similar escapade after the caning. I asked him why he hadn't just got rid of her after her infidelity, and he answered that it was so difficult to find women who like to be spanked. He no doubt loved her as well, but was considerate enough to omit that part of the story.

On another occasion, he had sent a girlfriend round to another man's house to be spanked by him as punishment for being an outrageous flirt at parties. She would kiss other men in front of him. I asked if he had enjoyed watching her being spanked by another man, and he said he hadn't been there, but he would have found out if she hadn't turned up for the spanking and given her double the punishment. After that, she apparently moderated her behaviour.

On the one hand, he sounded quite tolerant, continuing relationships with girls that seemed to be interested in other guys. On the other, it looked as if he could sometimes take what should be a fun, consensual, sexy pastime further than the normal spanking world intended by extending the boundaries to include serious corporal punishment.

I had to admit to myself that I'd had two extra-marital affairs, but that was after years of living with a liar, who contributed very little to household bills, while somehow managing to go motor racing on a regular basis, and with whom I hadn't had sex for many years. I would much rather have stayed with Pen had things been working out between us. So I convinced myself that, if a relationship developed between myself and Robin, I wouldn't want to be unfaithful anyway, and the caning issue wouldn't arise. Amazing what you tell yourself in the initial throes of love.

Nevertheless, I wasn't interested at all in a relationship where corporal punishment would be a constant serious threat. Any real disagreements or issues should be sorted out by discussion and listening to each other's point of view through mutual respect. I made him promise that he would never use the cane on me for discipline. This wasn't boarding school. After a little persuasion, he promised, although I wasn't convinced of his sincerity.

We arranged for him to come to my house. It just seemed sensible to try out our newly-found interest in a safe environment. I met him at the motorway service station near my home. We'd agreed that we would both be nervous before meeting again but that, within a few minutes, we would be fine.

It took him an hour and a half to drive up from Brenwyth. I hadn't realised he lived that far from me. It would make this a 'long-distance relationship', which is never a good start. We drove to the nearby pub to have lunch, which was a much more relaxed affair than the first date. Once you know someone is a spanker, it breaks the ice. We hurried through the meal, realising that we couldn't wait to get back to my house and start spanking, most likely leading to sex.

As soon as we walked in the door, he grabbed me and hauled me over his knee on the sofa. I was wearing a knee-length tight green khaki dress, but he soon had this up over my bottom and wasted no time in starting to spank me. The boundaries between second date and spanker blurred, and very quickly he pulled my knickers down to my knees. It was the first time a normal date had become a spanking session, and it felt very natural. Blue had been a spanker and then become a sort of date, although the dating side had been definitely one-sided (my side). Maybe with Robin, the dating and spanking would work nicely in parallel, one feeding off the other.

'Take this off,' he suddenly commanded, tugging at my dress. And there it was – a dominant personality appearing, as with all the other spankers I'd come across. I would have to decide how much I liked to be ordered around by a boyfriend. I knew from my experience with Blue that it was all part of the erotic, punishment-based theme surrounding CP, and it could be a magnificently tantalizing arrangement if I could only surrender to it.

What was holding me back? I didn't mind being ordered around by client spankers. That was what they paid for. But being bossed around by a boyfriend went against the grain. What happened to women's lib? That's nothing to do with it, I could hear Blue shouting in my ear. 'Outside the CP scenario, you can be as liberated as you like,' he would have said. 'Just don't ruin this amazingly erotic opportunity with ego and old-hat emancipation ideas. If he starts trying to control you outside the bedroom, deal with that separately. Let him be your dom and dive right into this new spanking sex life with all your heart.'

I didn't have long to think about it. The dress came off, the knickers were already off, and then he quickly removed my bra, and we went upstairs for what promised to be our first erotic session. He put me over his knee again over the bed and continued spanking me.

'You're taking this well,' he commented, 'shall I show you a real spanking?'

'Er – go on then.'

He gave me three very hard slaps in succession, but my skin was so thick from previous spankings that it was no problem for me to endure a short, hard volley like that one.

'If you've got a belt, go and get it,' he ordered. I liked the belt, as long as I kept my legs together so that a stray end couldn't strike my lips by mistake, which could sting. I found a belt and handed it to him with some excitement and trepidation. He immediately doubled it up and started slapping my bottom with it while I was still over his knee. It stung quite a bit, but I was loving it. Spanking and dating all in one.

We got into bed, excited at the thought of our first sexual encounter. But quite soon after we started, Robin's stomach began to rumble and it became apparent that the pub food hadn't agreed with him. He was having problems emptying his bladder, and an erection never materialised. But it was still nice lying naked with this huge, gorgeous man in my bed and feeling quite at home with him.

After about two hours, he had to leave in order to fulfil a work request for a customer. I felt sure we would meet again. He seemed so keen, but sensibly so, not irritatingly so.

The next day I received a text thanking me for the lunch and saying how much he'd enjoyed the afternoon. As usual, there was no mention of meeting up again, but I was now accustomed to this, even if I didn't like it. If this relationship doesn't work out, I said to myself, I'm not going to agree to meet anyone else further than thirty minutes away from my house.

By a dreadful quirk of timing, I had planned to be busy for the next four weekends, helping my mother leave the family home of sixty years in the West Country and move into a residential home in the Midlands, where my younger sister and I lived. My father had died peacefully at home six years earlier at the age of ninety-two, and my mother had rattled around in the large, four-bedroomed house by herself since that time, becoming more and more isolated as her friends died one by one. It was time for her to live near her family.

Four weekends to be unavailable after a second date is not conducive to romance. When I told Robin, his half-joking reply was a surprised, 'Are you trying to avoid me?' For his part, he seemed too busy during the week to meet up. I could see this little relationship going down the pan before it had really started.

We texted each other sometimes, but although he initiated some of the conversations, most were about spanking, and no date was mentioned by him. I suggested we could go body-surfing and/or visit a wind tunnel and/or go for a posh meal. He readily agreed to all three ideas but was never available on the dates I suggested and never suggested alternative dates for these activities.

In our first chat about spanking he had mentioned living together, but I had assumed he was just talking out loud, in the first rush of finding someone even vaguely compatible. I couldn't see him wanting to move away from Brenwyth on the coast, away from his passion for sailing, to the landlocked Midlands, and at that point, I had no intention of moving to Wales. In actual fact, I didn't really want to live with anyone again if I could help it.

I decided to push for one more date. If he didn't seem interested enough after that to even try and meet up by taking the initiative for once, I would tell him yet again that I was 'happy to leave it'.

I decided four weekends on the trot to help arrange goodbye parties for my mother was too much. My two sisters could cope without me. So I cancelled one of them and told Robin I was free for that third weekend. I didn't hear anything for the whole of the next week, and then on the Saturday morning, ten days after the second date, he finally sent a text suggesting we meet for lunch at Symonds Yat, and then go for a walk. I was pleased that it was a normal date, and had nothing to do with spanking. This third date was now his idea, and he couldn't feel that I was pressuring him.

We met up and had lunch by the river Wye. I started to realise that he was quite a shy bloke when it came to people he didn't know, and relationships. He said he was happy to pay for lunch, and that I could pay next time. Then he suddenly shot me a nervous glance. 'If we are saying there's going to be a next time?' he added.

I assured him there would be.

We took a canoe and paddled up the river. It was a beautiful day and we chatted and laughed all the way up the river and all the way back down, especially when he realised I wasn't doing much paddling. Neither of us mentioned spanking.

By the end of the third date, I knew we had a real opportunity here. He had a zest for life and new experiences that matched my own. He was an intelligent, calm, quietly-confident individual who maintained that to hold grudges was to only harm yourself. He didn't criticise me, and he didn't say an unkind word about anyone he knew. The mutual desire to spank was the icing on the cake.

But given the distance between Robin and me, our respective working hours and time-consuming hobbies (his sailing and my tennis), his propensity for no communication, I considered a relationship fairly unlikely, but not impossible if both of us were prepared to fight for it. For my part, I intended to put the effort and hours in, at least initially, as long as I could detect a reciprocal interest from him.

I realised something else. Even though Robin had generously stated that he wouldn't mind my continuing with my spanking exploits, I knew if the right man came along (possibly Robin) that I would give up being a spankee, except privately for him. I thought it would be unfair to ask any man to put up with a girlfriend being spanked naked and touched by other men. Relationships are hard enough without engendering imagined scenarios with a third party and unnecessary jealousies.

I couldn't help asking him how often he thought a couple should see each other since it seemed he was happy with once every two or three weeks. He explained that May and June were extremely busy months for the garden equipment business. After that, he maintained, he would want to see me once or twice a week, even given the distance. It turned out he had in fact tried to text me on occasion, but his new flat was located in a depression, and sometimes the texts were returned undelivered. Also, he reminded me, wasn't I the one who had planned to be unavailable for four consecutive weekends?

*****

In a Hollywood film…

Robin and I would have found a little cottage halfway between Brenwyth and Chorton Common, and moved in together. He would have continued to sail, and I would have carried on playing tennis. Our sex life, immersed in spankings, beltings and the odd gentle caning, would have always ended in instant synchronous orgasms…

*****

And this is what really happened. Within a month, the same pattern was emerging. Our lives were either too busy or he was too far away with his work to meet up. No one was to blame. We even started saying things like 'If only we lived nearer,' and 'If only you sailed'. Over the next year we only managed to see each other three more times, with months in between.

By the second of the three final dates, I told him I was already looking on the dating sites for someone else, but that I was still very interested in him if we could find more time to meet up somehow. He said he understood but still wanted to meet up. So one night we had a quick drink in a nearby pub and then went for a walk in the dark. We had a quick spank over the car bonnet and, as I was getting turned on, I invited him to have sex.

'I don't want to do it like this. We will have the opportunity to do it properly soon,' he said, more sensibly than I wanted him to be.

'What if we never have another chance?' I asked him as my only line of persuasion.

'We definitely will.'

Two months later, I had met someone else on one of the dating sites. I wasn't sure about him, but my interest in Robin was beginning to falter anyway. With such large gaps between dates, the chemistry between us was waning. On our last date, we went for a walk, and it was then that I decided that I couldn't keep waiting for him. The other guy lived fifteen minutes away from me, and in the first week, we had seen each other five times. A slight difference from six dates in a year.

Robin will always be the one that got away. A lost opportunity. He texted me every now and then over the next five years, but the texts were again mainly about spanking. We managed to have two brief non-date drinks during that time. Each time he asked me if I was still with the guy from the dating site. Each time I confirmed that I was, and he said he wished he had done more to keep me when he had the chance. He reiterated that it was so hard to find women who wanted to spank. I didn't want him to wait for me, so I made it easier for him. I let him know (truthfully) that I had come off HRT and with it had gone my libido and any real desire for spanking. I never heard from him again.

Chapter 21

Love and Spanking

The 'guy from the dating site' was called Nick. He was 59, like me, virtually bald (unlike me), with a white, goatee beard (I disliked goatee beards intensely), slim and 5' 11" tall. He seemed slightly suntanned in his profile photo and looked rather exotic, as if he came from Siberia, since he had slightly slanting eyes. He turned out to be as English as they come, with an upper-middle-class accent prevalent in English boarding schools. He lived in the nearby city and played tennis, according to his profile. Intriguing, and rather good-looking.

I wondered what he did for a living. I was not going to have a relationship with anyone who couldn't at least pay halves in a restaurant or weekend breaks or foreign holidays. I was relieved to see he had been the manager of his own catering business for the previous thirty years.

So I contacted him on the dating site.

'Hi Nick,
You look rather nice. I see you play tennis and live near me. If you like my profile at all, it would be very nice to hear from you.
Anna.'

I waited a week. Then two weeks. No reply. So I reluctantly started looking at other profiles, but none had piqued my interest as Nick's had done, especially given the common interest of tennis. After a few weeks on this site, I thought I'd try a different site.

Anyone who has tried online dating will know that you often see the same old faces on different sites. And why not? It just extends your choices, since there are normally a few different people on other sites whom you haven't seen before. Some people dare to put different names and ages to different or even the same photos of themselves on each site, although it's fairly obvious and really just gives the impression that they are prepared to be dishonest, which is not a good start to a new and budding relationship.

I recognised Nick's profile again on this site. It was a different photo, but I was glad to see the details were the same as on the other site. He was sitting in a deck chair, wearing a white shirt, which showed off his broad chest. I pretended to be unsure if I had contacted him previously. What was I saying about being honest? I thought this type of white lie would be allowed in the social ethics of dating sites.

'*Hi Nick,*
Sorry if I've contacted you before. I do like your profile so if you like mine at all it would be very nice to hear from you. We live near each other and both like tennis.
Anna.'

This time I received a reply.

'*Anna hi,*
Shall we go for a coffee?
Nick'

Blimey! That was an abrupt turnaround. But I liked the decisiveness and lack of trying to email for weeks before meeting. Quite right. Why not just get down to meeting quickly, instead of wasting hours of each other's time. And what a difference from Robin, who took days or even weeks to answer one text.

I immodestly assumed at the time when I saw Nick's email that he had missed my original email and then on my second email thought how sexy and stunning I was. Yes, that must be it. That was not the case at all, as I found out later. At the time of the first email, Nick was just splitting up with his girlfriend of eleven years and was trying to find a place of his own. The relationship had descended into shouting matches, mostly on her side, and Nick's nerves were shredded. He had only gone onto the first dating site to put a marker down that he was back in the 'market' and to reassure himself that there was indeed a world out there and he had a future in that world. It made him feel better – without really being interested at all in meeting anyone. He had seen my first email but didn't have the mental energy to answer it. When he received my second email, he recognised me straight away, and thought 'Well, why not? It can't do any harm.' But he was not interested in getting to know me first, hence the brusque invitation for coffee.

'Could I phone you first?' I replied. *'I don't normally meet people without talking to them first.'*

'It will be fine,' came back the immediate reply.

Hmmm. This guy either didn't brook arguments or he couldn't be bothered to speak to me first. So instead of saying what was on my mind, which was, 'Listen, mate, I'm not fucking meeting you without talking to you first.' I adopted a softly, softly, humorous approach.

'Er, well just in case you're a bandit or a nutter, I would prefer to talk to you first.'

He was amused by this, and eventually sent me his mobile number. I rang it. The most gorgeous soft male voice, with a neutral southern-English educated accent, said, 'Hi. Is that Anna?' I have since likened his voice to liquid gold. I've even encouraged him to try and do voice-overs for TV, films or radio, with no success. After a minute long conversation, I had made up my mind.

'Oh you sound fine. Let's go for that coffee.'

But he seemed to want to talk some more. The conversation lasted another five minutes and it was obvious we had the same sense of humour. I remember saying that I was glad my husband was dead, or I would have lost the house because of his debts. He laughed out loud at this. The coffee date idea was abandoned. It turned into a drink in the nearby pub in the evening a few days later.

During the drink, we seemed to get on well. He was one of the few guys to look exactly like his profile. We both remember laughing a lot during the evening. At one point, he stared right into my eyes for a few seconds. I didn't know what to do so I looked away, making a joke that he seemed to be looking into my soul. He laughed and said, 'I know.' He told me afterwards that he had done this on purpose to see my reaction and because he felt there could be quite a deep connection between us.

We saw each other five times that week. I saw his new flat, which had an enormous lounge with only one tiny, old shabby sofa in it, salvaged from his previous house. You would think the relationship would have soared high and deep from such a promising start. But it didn't. He was still in love with his girlfriend and wanted to resolve many issues with her. He very obviously didn't have closure with her, and it was hard for him to concentrate on a new relationship with me. I was still wondering about Robin and whether I should still wait for the next date, which would no doubt be weeks away.

But even though neither Nick nor I were sure about our relationship, it somehow just continued on its own way, since it was nicer to have someone to go out with than no one. I think we were both just lonely and lost, and it was nice to have someone to snuggle up with, even if it wasn't quite the first choice. I had met forty-four other men from the two dating sites. For all sorts of reasons, they were not suitable for me. I was fairly resigned and mentally tired from having my hopes raised and dashed each time, so it was a relief to meet someone halfway decent and vaguely compatible.

We slept together about a month after meeting. We were both slightly embarrassed, and got through it with only a modicum of success. There were no orgasms, quite a lot of fumbling, and I think we were glad when it was all over. Of course, as usual, the sex got better over time when we were more familiar with each other, but we were both still only going through the motions of having a relationship. I didn't dare mention spanking. He might have run a mile.

About two months later, with both of us wavering about whether to continue the relationship, Nick told me his son, aged about 19 at the time, asked him how he was getting on with me.

'I really don't know,' he had answered. 'I don't know how I feel about her, and I don't know how she feels about me.'

We had first met on October 19th, and now we were coming up to New Year's Eve. I decided to wait until after the new year to broach the subject of whether we should continue. He invited me to his house to see in the new year. He cooked us a lovely meal and then suddenly took me by the hand and led me to his bedroom. The light from dozens of candles placed all around the room shone out from the darkness. My heart melted, and we snuggled in bed into the new year, drinking Prosecco, eating chocolates and watching the rubbish New Year's Eve programmes on TV.

I don't know why such a simple, sweet gesture would have swayed me as it did. Maybe it was the fact that he had made such an effort for me when I had assumed that he still felt so much for his previous girlfriend. The other reason was that I had recently been on my final walk with Robin and had been rather relieved to realise that this long-distant relationship would never have worked. I turned to my new relationship with Nick with renewed enthusiasm and hope.

Not long after New Year, we decided to go away for the weekend. We stayed in a hotel in a small town about an hour away. The idea was just to have a break, have a few cosy meals, and take a few explorative walks round the town. Our sex life had been improving gradually, and we no longer felt embarrassed in front of each other. Ironic that I had been quite happy to take off all my clothes, bend over and spread my legs in front of countless strange men, but a new unfamiliar boyfriend was a different matter. Much more critical that he liked my body, and that we felt intimate. Which we were beginning to do.

Nick felt our closeness too. So much so that during the weekend away, he felt able to tell me one of his darkest secrets. I was taking a shower and he came and joined me. We had a lovely, lingering kiss as the warm water cascaded down over us. We felt sexy and, wrapped in towels, moved to the bed. But instead of taking me in his arms, Nick just lay beside me and said he wanted to tell me something.

He had been abused as a child at boarding school. He was having a piano lesson when the music teacher suddenly put his hand down the front of his trousers as he sat at the piano and began to play with him. He was eleven years old and couldn't take in or understand what was happening. He and the teacher never discussed it, but it kept happening. He was of an era where well-brought-up little boys didn't question adults' behaviour. He didn't tell his parents either. He dreaded going back to school after the holidays, and is now surprised that neither of his parents suspected anything. He also dreaded the piano lessons but kept going because that's what you did aged eleven if your teachers demanded it, especially back in the 1960s.

I didn't know anything about abuse. My initial thoughts as he told his tale was that it was indeed dreadful and must have affected him for a time, but that now he was an adult and it was many years later, he would obviously have been able to move on, put it to one side, and regard it as an unlucky event in his past.

Not so. Not by any stretch of the imagination. Abuse like this has far-reaching consequences and nearly always affects people their entire lives. They sometimes cannot have successful relationships as their attitude to sex has been drastically distorted and damaged. The child often feels what Nick calls 'toxic shame' for letting the perpetrator do, and continue to do, such depraved acts. He doesn't know why he didn't stop him. He wonders if he secretly enjoyed it; otherwise, he would have put an end to it, right? Wrong. An eleven-year-old boy trusts adults. If an adult carries out this act, it must be the right thing to do, so he wouldn't question it, especially in a situation where he wants to learn a skill from the adult. Nick just wanted to learn the piano.

The other consequence of such despicable acts on a defenceless, trusting child is inducing an anger that won't go away. The perpetrator has taken their childhood. Abused children can't go back to their blissful state of ignorance before the abuse. It makes them feel different from other children. It makes them feel bewildered, fearful, unconfident and, above all, untrusting in their hitherto safe world. And alone. Nick didn't tell anyone, even though he knew instinctively that what happened was somehow 'not right'. He couldn't tell other adults because they would blame him, wouldn't they? Or not believe him. What a sad burden for an eleven-year-old. Especially one at boarding school, away from his parents for weeks at a time. The piano teacher was well aware of this fact and took full advantage.

There's also an abiding resentment that the abuser has somehow had control of their lives long after the abuse itself is over, and the abuser no longer even around. Whatever abuse victims are made to feel as a child often extends to similar feelings as a teenager and adult. Nick told me that the abuse created considerable confusion in his teens as to his sexual identity which took years to resolve itself. Even though victims realise as an adult that it was not their fault as a child, the 'toxic shame' at what happened, and the rage at the thought of their lives being damaged, and often ruined, by some cowardly pervert, haunts many of them to the end of their days.

The BBC *Victoria Derbyshire* TV programme highlighted an abuse issue among young boys wishing to learn football and being continually abused by their football coach. The victims, now adults in their forties, cried openly on the programme as they described the effect the abuse had had, and was still having, on their lives.

I lay on the bed and listened to Nick opening his heart to me. I felt honoured that he wanted to share this secret with me, and trusted me with it. But to be honest, I wondered at the time in my ignorance why he was telling me with such seriousness, why he had taken so long to tell me; in short, why it seemed to be such a big deal to him. Only over the next few months and years did I come to realise the devastating effect of abuse on its victims. It was probably a good thing that I didn't know much about it because it might have changed my attitude to having sex with him. I may have tried to pity him or been on tenterhooks around him during sex, which is the last thing he would have wanted.

As it was, we just carried on with our sexual lives as before. I still hadn't dared to mention spanking. It wasn't because of the abuse that I didn't mention it. It was because I didn't want him to think I was weird. I remembered Jeremy's story of telling one of his girlfriends about his desire to spank and he never saw her again. One of my school friends had told me she had encouraged a new boyfriend to whip her on the backs of her legs with a whip. She had told him how she enjoyed feeling the welts afterwards. He indulged her fetish for a few minutes and then suddenly rushed out of the flat, and never contacted her again.

But it didn't seem to matter. Nick and I seemed to be getting closer, to the point where something happened to us that we can't explain. It had never happened to either of us before, either with each other or with anyone else, and unfortunately it has never happened again, although we would love it to.

I was taking a shower in his flat and Nick came to join me. We had both finished washing, and had a few kisses. We were about to get out of the shower when I reached up for a final kiss. Something took hold between us, as if we had suddenly entered another universe. We both felt it at exactly the same time. It happened *to* us.

We didn't choose it and we had no control over it. I remember saying 'What was that?' Nick was as startled as I was and just looked at me with the same questioning look.

We moved to the bed and we estimate that 'it' continued there for about twenty minutes. We felt as if we were in our own little bubble, our own time warp, cocooned from the outside world. Afterwards, for want of better words, we could only describe it as our souls meeting spiritually somewhere in the ether.

During those twenty minutes, we continued to have sex, staring into each other's eyes, bewildered, filled with a sense of wonder and closeness.

We had once tried tantra sex without much success. Tantra sex focuses on the spirituality between the partners, as well as the physical enjoyment of sexual activities. I think we had both been too self-conscious to feel the benefits. I'm not interested in religion, spirituality or meditation, so I was probably unwittingly stopping dear old tantra in its tracks. Give me just a quickie any day.

As we lay there in each other's arms, we became gradually aware that the strange bubble was beginning to disappear. To this day, we wonder what happened. We would love it to come back but we feel we have no control over it except to keep a close and loving relationship. We refer to it as 'the thing'. Nick thinks it will happen again. I doubt that it will. I think it happened because we were in the throes of new love, which can be a feeling of overwhelming closeness, a time of extremely heightened senses and awareness of each other. Unfortunately, in my experience, that doesn't normally last.

Nick and I had no intention of moving in together for a very long time, if at all. His son, aged nineteen, had moved into his flat, which was within walking distance of the centre of a large, bustling city, perfect for a very good-looking, sociable boy. I was still getting used to living alone three years after Pen had died, and I was rather enjoying it. I could watch any TV programme I wanted, without anyone talking through it. I could leave the washing-up overnight. I was continuing my job as a full-time software developer and now had more money than I had probably ever had in my life. The household bills had halved and there was no one to suddenly request £300 for a bill he couldn't pay.

Nick and I saw each other mostly at weekends but phoned each other often during the week. In the normal course of catch-up conversations after a few days apart, Nick would ask me what I had been doing. In the end, I had to tell him that I was writing my first autobiography, *Out of the Red*, because otherwise I felt he would have wondered what on earth I was doing with my free time. I suppose I could have just not mentioned it and concentrated on my many other interests – 'ceroc' dancing, tennis, badminton, photography, cinema, meeting friends – but one part of me wanted to let him know about the spanking. For eighteen months in the very recent past, spanking had been a big part of my life.

I had, in fact, stopped such activity, as it did entail a lot of intimate touching, and I didn't think it would have been fair to Nick to continue behind his back, or even with his knowledge. I had probably made between £5000 and £6000 in spanking revenues over the eighteen months. My mother, widowed with all Dad's money, had helped me with my mortgage – by paying it off. So I was in a much more secure financial situation and could afford the reduction in income, even with the continuing payments towards the £20,000 debt left me by my dear husband.

The text of the book was still in draft form, but nearing completion, and Nick asked if he could read it to give an overall opinion before it went to print. I hesitated. Halfway through writing the book, I had started the spanking exploits. I had told the publishers, and they had jumped at the chance, stating that it would very likely help sell the book. They wanted to add the subtitle '*Spanked for Profit and Pleasure*' to any title I chose. So the second half of the book was very much about spanking, and Nick couldn't help notice my salacious secret even by the title. I also wondered if he might be a secret spanker, or if not, interested in trying it out. It didn't occur to me that his earlier abuse might make him baulk at the idea.

'The thing is,' I ventured, 'it reveals rather a salacious secret, and I don't know what you will make of it.'

'OK, try me,' said Nick immediately, with his normal decisiveness.

But I couldn't bring myself to tell him for two days. During this time, we happened to meet at the theatre for a meal and a play. As soon as he joined me in the lobby, he said, 'Tell me what this secret is. It's driving me mad.'

Then he innocently added a sentence which any spanker would knowingly use to set up a punishment scenario. 'It's naughty of you not to tell me.'

I pretended not to have noticed his unwitting CP verbiage but was secretly pleased that he might have the makings of a natural dom. But I couldn't tell him before the play in case he walked off in horror.

So the next time he came through the door of my house, I said that I was ready to tell him. He sat at one end of the sofa and I at the other. I took a deep breath.

'I am, or was until very recently, a spankee. I was getting spanked by men for money.'

Nick's eyes widened. He had a look of astonishment on his face.

'Ooohh,' he eventually said. 'I'd thought of all sorts of things – prostitution, escorting, pornographic filming, but never spanking. Did it hurt?'

'Yes, sometimes. Especially the cane. But your bum becomes hardened to it. I don't do it now.'

Thankfully he was just intrigued. He wanted to know all about it. I think because I was no longer doing it, it didn't threaten him, and because I assured him there had been no sexual intercourse involved, he didn't seem to look at me with disgust. He thought I was very brave and said he would be very interested to read my book.

After duly reading the book from start to finish, Nick agreed with my fear that the book was one of two halves. The first half all about my ordinary life, which would interest no one but a handful of people. The second half all about spanking, and readers interested in CP wouldn't be interested in my life. But I wanted to leave the book as it was. I felt the need to 'get my life out there'. It had been cathartic to write about my painful attempts to get pregnant. Eight unsuccessful cycles of IVF were financially and emotionally draining. Pen and I had just started surrogacy arrangements when he died, and the surrogacy organisation had to pull out since they couldn't sanction a surrogate baby being donated to a single woman. I had considered adoption, but given the tight age restrictions imposed on adoption in the UK (at that time, there could be no more than 45 years between adoptive parent and child) I would have had to adopt a child aged about 14. Through no fault of his/her own, the poor child might well have had personality or mental issues, and I couldn't face that.

I couldn't tell anyone what had happened. I didn't want to burden them with a tale of woe, and I didn't want to appear a victim. And it was too painful to talk about anyway. I was afraid I would break down in front of my hapless listener. So I put it in a book. Even with all names disguised, it felt good that it was in the public domain.

My book went to print. My publisher helped me with contacts who could help with advertising and promotion, with the result that there was a flurry of interest from the media. The headline '*Woman has bottom spanked in order to pay for IVF*' appeared in one tabloid. '*Woman pays off late husband's debts by having her bottom spanked.*' was featured in another.

By clever marketing, the book made the 'bestsellers' list on *Amazon*. A book apparently only has to reach the top 100 for one hour in its chosen category for the author to be allowed to say the book is a 'bestseller'. A rather obscure category was chosen for me, and the book reached position 22. Had it reached the top of the category I could have proudly claimed my book was a 'No 1 bestseller'.

An ITV drama programme contacted me saying they were interested in producing a drama about my life. I was thrilled. Within a month, they wrote again to say they couldn't find any channels willing to take on such a project. Then a film company contacted me to say they were interested in making a film of my life. A contract was even drawn up between us. About a year later I realised I hadn't heard anything, so I contacted them. They said they'd found out during the year that another film depicting a woman with a similar life story had already been made, so they had ditched mine. Thanks for telling me.

In the meantime, my relationship with Nick was continuing to develop. We were having fun playing tennis, going for meals and walks, and we were getting to know each other's families. Our sex life was more relaxed, and we enjoyed exploring different positions and techniques. No spanking was mentioned, even though Nick now knew all about my past.

One weekend we had the house to ourselves. We were lying in Nick's big wooden double bed, watching TV, when we started to get amorous.

'Why don't you spank me?' I asked nonchalantly, trying to sound as if it wasn't a big deal.

'Er – I don't think I could. I wouldn't want to hurt you,' he replied, slightly embarrassed.

'You don't have to do it hard, and, anyway, I'm used to it, so it would be difficult to make it too painful. Just try it once. The whole idea is that it hurts a bit because it's supposed to be a punishment.'

I placed myself across his lap, presenting my bare bottom to his right hand. After a while, I felt two little slaps then he stopped.

'I just can't. It feels like abuse.'

'It's not like that,' I assured him. 'I will enjoy it too.'

I felt two more half-hearted slaps on my bottom then he stopped again. I looked back at him from my horizontal position. I was surprised to see sweat pouring off his face, chest and arms; he felt cold to the touch and looked very uncomfortable. I extricated myself from over his lap and lay beside him. It was beginning to dawn on me that the abuse long ago might be reaching out from the past to affect him.

'Are you alright?'

'It doesn't feel right. I don't want to hurt you.'

'That's fine. We can try it another time.' I felt a bit stupid for having suggested it, and for having lain across his knee as if begging for punishment. In all the role-playing, it was always the male spanker who had 'created' the need for a spanking and conjured up the reason. Here there was no reason banded about, no punishment needed, which left two embarrassed adults.

We abandoned the idea of spanking for the next few weeks. Then we went away for a weekend to London and stayed in a hotel. We'd just been for a nice meal, and when we came back, having drunk a fair amount of alcohol, we fell on the bed together. I dared suggest he spank me again.

'OK,' he said, slightly reluctantly, 'lie over my knee.' This time he managed four or five slaps and then had to stop. Sweat poured off him again. His chest was matted with sweat, and he felt very cold again.

'I'll have to stop, I'm afraid.'

'No worries. We don't have to try it again at all if you don't want to.'

Over the next few weeks, I put myself across his knee when sex was not even on the agenda. Fully dressed and just for fun. That way, he felt no pressure to 'perform a spanking' during foreplay. Slowly and gradually, he began to spank me over my jeans without my goading him. He started reading about it on the internet and finding out why people did it. At one point, he said, 'Yes, I see – it seems to be for mutual enjoyment – pretend punishment.'

'Yes!' I exclaimed, delighted that he was even bothering to explore the subject.

One day he suddenly looked at me in a strange way in the sitting room. 'I think I get it.' Then a minute later, 'Come here. I've been very disappointed with your behaviour recently, and I'd like you over my knee – now.' He grabbed me, and I shrieked as he put me over his knee. He pulled my knickers down and began a gentle hand-spanking that gradually grew harder. The jeans and knickers came off, and we had very erotic sex over the armchair.

And so started a period of eroticism that I'd never experienced before. Nick surprised both of us by falling easily into the dominant role-play. In fact, he surpassed me by far in role-play. I made an attempt at being a rebel, but mainly just ended up laughing. This didn't phase him. He normally started by hauling me dressed over his knee for a hand-spanking then ordering me to undress fully and put myself face down on the nearby armchair with the electric foot extension extended, where I could lie spread-eagled, face down, or over the back of the armchair. He would continue to berate my wayward attitude throughout.

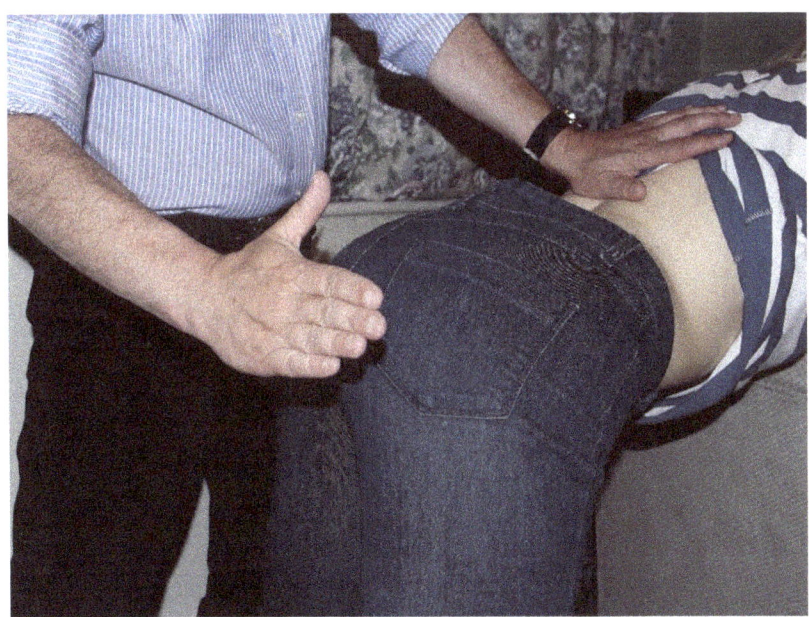

Hand spankings often started when I was fully dressed.

*Nick preferred hand-spanking to all other implements.
He said he enjoyed the hand-bottom contact.*

I had ordered a jumping bat (a padded riding crop), which made a lovely loud thwack but hardly stung at all.

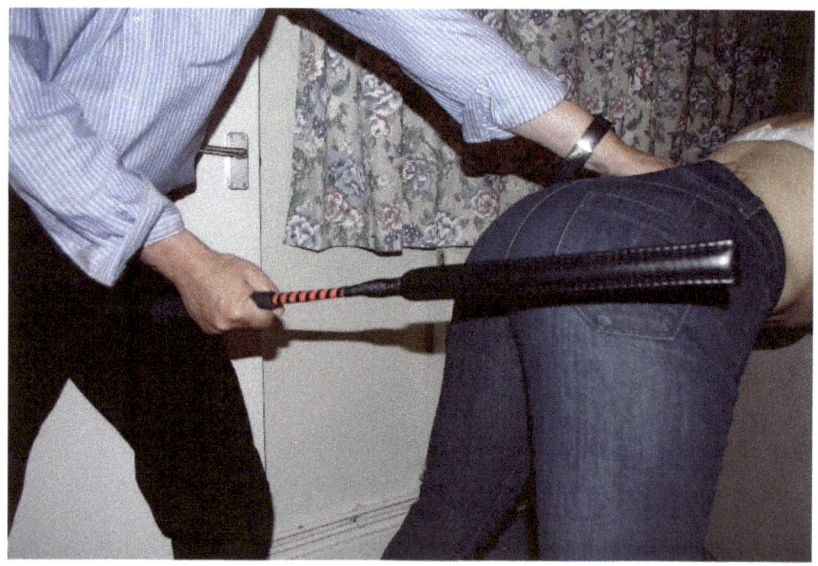

Nick liked to use the jumping bat, as it made a lovely loud thwack but hardly hurt at all, especially over jeans.

We also used a leather strap and a riding crop, just for variation.

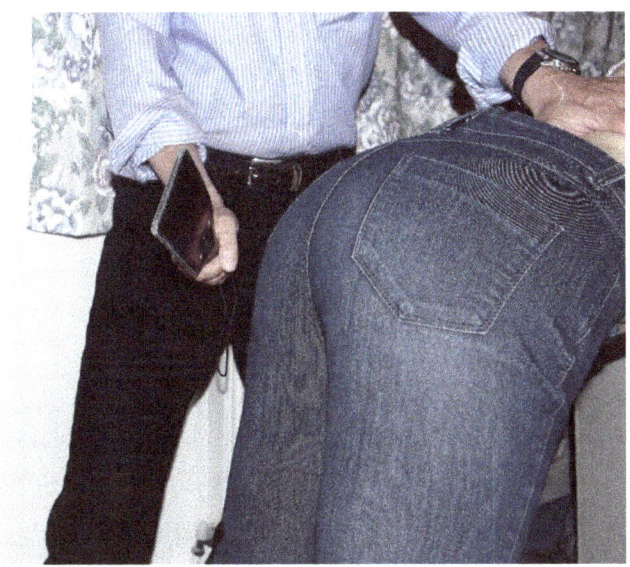

The leather strap was used occasionally, but mostly over jeans, otherwise I complained too much.

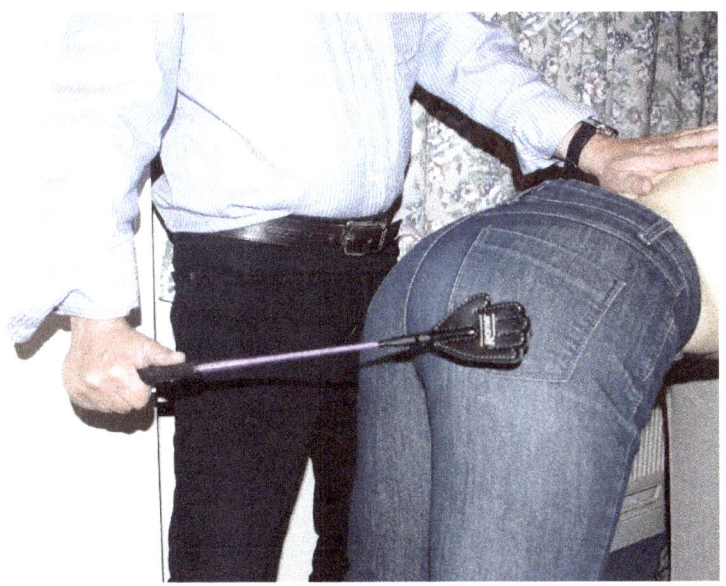

The riding crop was nice and bendy and didn't hurt too much,

especially over jeans.

Nick enjoyed using this as well as his belt. He would stand over me in feigned displeasure, slowly removing his belt so that I could watch. Occasionally, especially at the beginning, a stray belt end or crop would strike my vagina, and I would give a yelp, which reminded him that he hadn't asked me to close my legs. But soon, he learnt to whip one buttock and then the other, rather than whip across both buttocks at the same time, which can also hurt the vagina. After a while, he correctly targeted the lower half of the bottom as well, as other experienced spankers did. He tried the cane on me very gently a few times, but I decided the pain was not worth tolerating without the incentive of money. So after a lengthy spanking, belting or whipping, we would retire to the bedroom to have surprisingly erotic sex.

We also tried spanking outside but encountered the now-familiar problem of finding somewhere suitably secluded, comfortable enough for me, and at the right height for both of us.

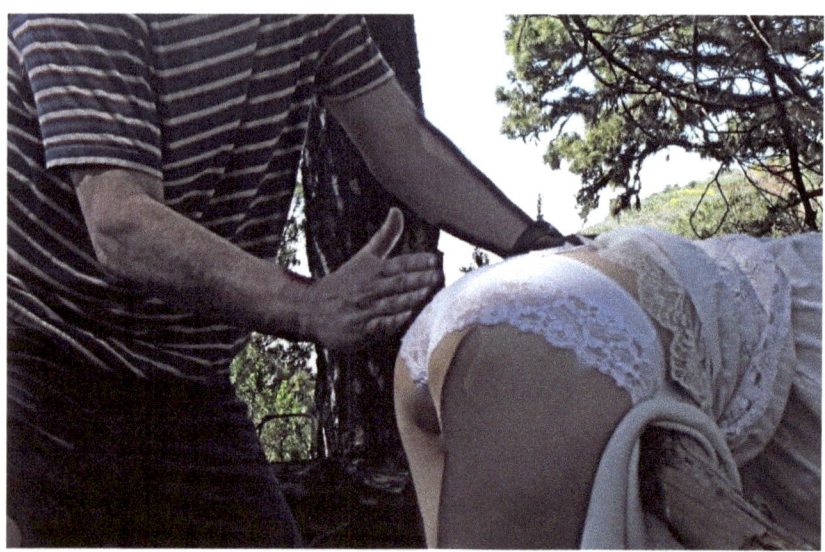

Finding a comfortable place to spank outside was often difficult.
Photo by Nick Turner.

We found a convenient tree trunk, but had this been for a paying spanker they would probably have found it too low, unless they had brought a riding crop or cane. Photo by Nick Turner.

We had bought a caravan between us, and it turned out to be an ideal place for spanking and punishment. After finding fault with everything I did, Nick would tie me to the bed, spread-eagled, face down, wallop me with a flip-flop that we kept permanently in a drawer there, and this would inevitably lead to sex. His enthusiasm once got the better of him. He was horrified to see one buttock start to bleed from the flip-flop strokes. He was mortified and apologised profusely. Apparently, if you cane someone enough to make them bleed, it can cause a weakness in the skin, which then has a tendency to bleed easily thereafter. Some spankees have had to give up the scene due to severe canings. (This is usually attributable to rogue solo players outside of the party community.) Knowing this, Nick and I were worried that it would keep bleeding too readily after that, and we might have to give up our newfound sexy activity, but it seemed to heal like any other abrasion, and we carried on undaunted.

A few weeks after he 'got it', we had an argument. I can't even remember what it was about now. I thought it was over, so I went into the bathroom to get ready for bed. He was already in bed, ostensibly reading but was, in fact, simmering with anger. I innocently came out of the bathroom in my dark blue silk nightie. I needed something from under my pillow, which was the other side of Nick, so I reached over him to try and find it. Within a trice, Nick pinned me down across his body and started spanking me quite hard over my nightie with his left hand, the only hand available. (He is right-handed.) I looked back at his face and was slightly alarmed to see that he was genuinely angry.

The spanking hurt. There had been no warm-up and it went on unabated for about ten seconds. I lay still, wondering how much harder it was going to be and how much longer it was going to last. Good thing it was his left hand, or it might have been too painful. He stopped and flung my legs round in a fit of temper so that I was lying on my front next to him.

No one spoke for a few seconds. Then I started laughing, and after a few moments, he joined in. It was the only 'proper' spanking I'd ever received, and am probably ever likely to receive, from a boyfriend. It was such a turn-on for both of us and led to a very sensual session of love-making. We laugh about it now, referring to it as 'the real spanking'.

A similar situation hasn't arisen since then. Nick said afterwards that although he found spanking me that time very sexy, it was obviously not an ideal way to solve problems between us. He said he was suddenly just so angry that he couldn't think of anything else to do, and when he saw my upturned bottom over his body, he couldn't help himself. But he wondered whether, if that happened too much, it would cross the line into abuse.

Nowadays, we don't argue much, but when we do, we try and resolve it by discussing the issues. I wonder if secretly I would like another real spanking? The problem is, I wouldn't want the accompanying anger from Nick. So the answer has to be a resounding 'No'. I'll stick to fun spankings for pretend punishment.

Chapter 22

Promoting the Book with my New Assistant Dom

About three months after my book came out, and the media interest had died down, I decided to contact one of the local newspapers. The female reporter hadn't been aware of my book and expressed a great deal of interest.

'Would you be able to send us a photo?' she asked.

I said I thought I could.

So one sunny day, Nick and I drove out into the countryside, wooden chair in the back seat, looking for the quintessential spanking field. We would both wear hats to disguise our faces. We found a field full of buttercups, enclosed by hedges on all sides. We plonked the chair in the middle of the field, set up the automatic camera to give us ten seconds to get in position, and started taking dozens of photos.

It was difficult to get the timing right. I had to wait for Nick to set up the camera, rush through the buttercups and grass and sit down on the chair before I could take up my position over his knee. All within ten seconds. It caused much hilarity. Some photos looked as if I was levitating on a layer of buttercups rather than over Nick's knee.

One of the first attempts to show a country spanking in the buttercup field. I look like I'm levitating so we couldn't use this photo.

In some, I looked as if I only had one leg. In others, our faces, especially Nick's, were too visible. But we eventually took the photo shown on page 201, which was used in the newspaper's weekend magazine, along with a page-long article about me (in the name of Anna J Skye) and the book. We bought a copy and went to a café to have a cup of tea and read the article. Nick chuckled to himself as he saw a photo of himself, spanking a woman in a white dress in a field, in a fairly widely-read magazine. Not your average holiday snap.

'Little did I know what I was getting myself into when I answered you on the dating site,' he laughed.

Promoting the first book in the buttercup field for a local newspaper. This photo appeared in the paper's weekend magazine.
Photo by Nick Turner.

We contemplated sending in more revealing photos, but in the end, we decided to emphasise the more fun side of spanking.

We decided against sending in this photo to the local newspaper, as we thought they might not be able to use it due to the risky content.
Photo by Nick Turner.']

We also decided against sending this photo to the local newspaper, as it was unlikely they could use it, due again to the sexy content.

Photo by Nick Turner.

The local radio contacted me. Would I do an interview over the phone? To begin with, I refused, but then considered it highly unlikely anyone I knew would either be listening, or recognise my voice if my name wasn't revealed. So I consented, as long as they disguised my name. On the day of the interview, I went to the publishers' offices so that I didn't have to give out my landline or mobile number to the radio producers. I was shown into a tiny back office with a desk and phone on it. The interview was in five minutes, and I suddenly became aware of an enormous bluebottle flying round the tiny room. No way could I give an interview with that thing buzzing round my face, so I opened the door to let it out. It would not leave. I dashed down the corridor, looking for the guy who had let me in. He quickly came in and chased it out. The phone rang about fifteen seconds after he had closed the door behind him.

A very friendly, articulate woman introduced herself. She explained that it was not a live interview, so I was not to worry if I said anything I regretted, as they could just record that part again. And then she launched into the interview. She asked very pertinent questions as a lay vanilla person, and I was quite enjoying myself, explaining about the secret world of corporate punishment, which few people would know first-hand or understand. She particularly wanted to know about the implements used, how much each one hurt, whether I was ever bruised, and whether spankers sometimes refused to stop if you asked them. To the latter question, I answered that it hadn't happened to me personally but that I'd heard that it did very rarely occur. I added that it probably only happened when the spanker was new to the scene and thought CP was all about pain and dominance, rather than mutual fun for spanker and spankee alike, within the spankee's tolerance levels.

At one point, she asked me how much I thought I had earned in the eighteen months. For some reason, I panicked, totted up roughly what I thought it would have been, and blurted out, 'About £12,000.'

There was a silence the other end, and I felt that she hadn't believed me. She was correct. I calculated it afterwards, and it would have probably come to between £5000 and £6000. I was charging £100 an hour, and managed a session only about three or four times a month because of the need for any bruising to heal.

Just when I was realising how much more there was to reveal about this fascinating subject, she suddenly said, 'We'll leave it there,' and added kindly, 'I feel I know you as a friend now. That was very interesting. Good luck with the book.'

We had spoken for about twenty minutes but they only used five minutes of the interview when it was aired two weeks later.

A well-known tabloid newspaper offered me 'a large sum' to do a piece on my story, if I agreed to have my photo taken and my name revealed. I never found out how much the sum was, as it was discussed through my publicist. I could have done with the money but decided that I couldn't risk someone recognising me and telling my mother and/or friends and/or more importantly my work, so I declined.

Nick started to enjoy his new role as Assistant-Dom-Photographer. He bought me a string body stocking and set about taking photos, the best of which are below. We weren't quite sure what we were going to use them for, but it was fun trying to look the most spankable I could possibly look, just for the hell of it.

One of my most spankable poses. Photo by Nick Turner.

Another spankable, sexy position. Photo by Nick Turner.

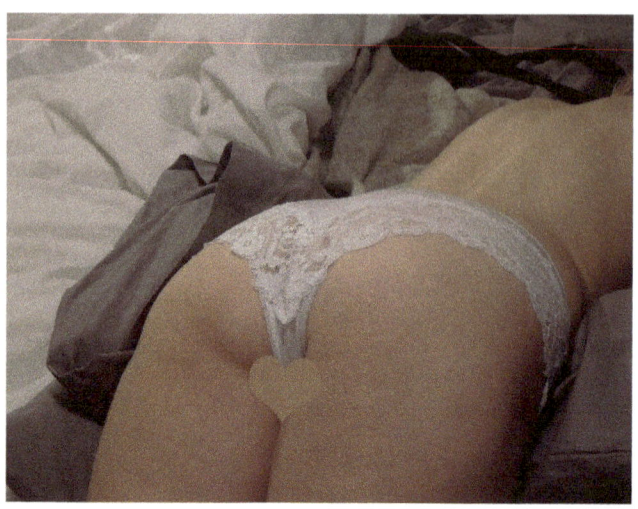

Another spankable pose. Photo by Nick Turner.

Nick and I became bold. We ventured outside again to try and take some tasteful, artistic photos. Not to promote the book necessarily, but just because we could.

We would, however, have been pleased to forward any of the photos to the media had they requested it.

*Taken in a forest in the same lacy white dress as on the initial Spankee****** website. The colour sepia was used for atmospheric effect. Photo by Nick Turner.*

*Taken in the forest again, with the colour sepia overlaid.
Photo by Nick Turner.*

The same shot, only in black and white. Photo by Nick Turner.

We tried some shots with only my jeans down, with mixed results.

Photo by Nick Turner.

Photo by Nick Turner.

A dubious pose in a rape field. Photo by Nick Turner.

We made a video of me bending over the bonnet of Nick's car in a short, yellow, summer dress, with my back to the camera, wearing a large, floppy straw hat to disguise me. In later takes we remembered to drape a scarf across the number plate, but in the first few takes, such as the one in Photo 29, in our enthusiasm we forgot this rather crucial prop. Nick, adorned with a tilley hat, entered stage left. He walked straight up to me, placed his hand on my buttocks and gave me 5 or 6 hard slaps, then walked back out of shot. We posted it on a well-known web site with the name of the book on the label below the video. Within a few months we had over 100,000 hits.

Promoting the first book, with our first spanking video.

We became even more brazen. We took a self-shot video of me in the same yellow summer dress, bending over at right angles and leaning against a large tree in a field. My face was turned away from the camera under the same large, brimmed hat. Nick entered stage left again, walked up to me and started walloping me over my dress with a flip-flop. He didn't hold back. He had got the hang of this spanking idea by then, and you could see clearly the reverberation of each stroke on my dress. Then he lifted my dress and continued the walloping over my knickers. With the camera still whirring, he then pulled down my knickers and the flip-flop whipping continued on my bare bottom.

The first stage of the flip-flop spanking video, over my dress.

The second stage of the flip-flop spanking video, over my knickers.

The third stage, part 1, of the flip-flop spanking video, which we think is the reason we were banned.

The third stage, part 2, of the flip-flop spanking video. Nick enjoyed this form of punishment so much that it was tricky to get a still from the video as the flip-flop hardly stayed still long enough to appear without blurring.

I also posted this on the same website. We added some still shots of me wearing green galoshes up to my thighs, a white T-shirt, and another floppy hat, bending over a small bridge over a lovely stream. Nick stood behind me, wearing his tilley hat, left hand raised, about to strike. Soft, dreamy music played as the photos displayed one by one in a slideshow.

One of our favourite photos. Photo by Nick Turner.

One of the photos in the slideshow. Photo by Nick Turner.

Another photo in the slideshow. Photo by Nick Turner.

*Another tasteful hand-spanking against the tree for the slideshow.
Photo by Nick Turner*

We thought we'd got away with it, but about a month after this really quite rude video and slideshow was posted for the world to see, I went to take another look at it, as I was quite proud of the tasteful slideshow. I was met with a stark black and red error message: 'This item has been removed'. I subsequently received an email saying I had breached the decency rules of their site, and would not be able to display anything for another six months. I waited the six months but was met with the same terse message, so assumed I had been banned for good and gave up. Someone suggested I try posting it on one or more of the spanking sites, which I have yet to try.

Chapter 23

What Now?

Having got rid of all my debts, helped by the £5000-£6000 from the eighteen months as a spankee, I was able to retire a year ago from my job as a software developer. Aged 66 years, I am now looking forward to receiving my state pension.

I have no desire to go back to being a spankee. This is partly because I have a partner, and it wouldn't be fair to him. It's also partly because my body at 66 is definitely beginning to show its age, and I wouldn't want to see disappointment on spankers' faces. I am proud of myself for reducing my debts by being brave enough to meet strange men in hotel rooms. It now seems somehow normal but still somehow outrageous that I had the nerve to go through with this activity, but we can all surprise ourselves by overcoming fears and prejudices and achieving seemingly unreachable goals.

I still hear from several of the spankers whom I saw regularly and got to know on a personal basis. Some of them still wonder if I'm willing to arrange private spanking sessions with them, but when I decline these sometimes tempting offers, I'm delighted that they continue to keep in touch, telling me of their latest spanking exploits and other news.

Six and a half years later, Nick and I are still going strong. Three years ago, I had to come off HRT as the doctors told me there was an increased risk to health the longer I remained on it. My libido dropped away, and my desire for a spanking, although still sometimes in my head, has dramatically decreased. We still have the occasional spanking session, with or without sex, and the spark is still there, although it takes a little longer to ignite these days.

We have no intention of moving in together. We have both been put off by previous experiences of partners behaving in intolerable ways. We see each other mostly at weekends and have our own space during the week, which is the best of both worlds. He maintains jokingly that I corrupted him into the world of spanking, but I reckon he was a natural, waiting for the call. I tell him he's brought me over to the dark side – walking, my childhood pet hate. Like many people during the last eighteen months of the coronavirus pandemic, I've done more walking than during the whole of my life, and I've finally started to enjoy it.

I've found my 'someone to do nothing with'. Over the last six and a half years, Nick's been by my side, holding my hand walking by the sea, drinking wine by the fire and chatting about nothing and everything. My cup runneth over.

A kiss among the buttercups. Photo by Nick Turner.

References

The Naked Ape, Jonathan Cape Publishing, 1967.
Fifty Shades of Grey, Vintage Books, June 2011.
I Know Why the Caged Bird Sings, New York: Random House, 1969.

www.ingramcontent.com/pod-product-compliance
Lightning Source LLC
Chambersburg PA
CBHW041956080526
44588CB00021B/2765